# SAY IT MY WAY

# SAY IT MY WAY

How to Avoid Certain Pitfalls of Spoken English
Together with a Decidedly Informal History of
How Our Language Rose (or Fell)

## BY WILLARD R. ESPY

DOUBLEDAY & COMPANY, INC.
GARDEN CITY, NEW YORK
1980

The author and publisher gratefully acknowledge permission to include the following works:

"Brooklynese Champion," from *One to a Customer* by Margaret Fishback. Copyright 1933 by E. P. Dutton & Co., Inc. Renewal 1961 by Margaret Fishback Antolini. Reprinted by permission of the publisher, E. P. Dutton.

"Sonnet on Stewed Prunes," from *The Norsk Nightingale* by William F. Kirk. Reprinted by permission of the publisher, Dodd, Mead & Company.

Quotation by John K. Galbraith from the *Wall Street Journal*, reprinted by permission of John K. Galbraith.

"Words with One Syllable" by Joseph Ecclesine. Reprinted from the July 1961 *Reader's Digest*.

*The Serial* by Cyra McFadden. Reprinted by permission of the publisher, Alfred A. Knopf, Inc.

Excerpt from *The Complete Poems of Paul Laurence Dunbar* reprinted by permission of Dodd, Mead & Company, Inc.

*Do's Don'ts & Maybes of English Usage* by Theodore M. Bernstein. Copyright 1977 by Theodore M. Bernstein. Reprinted by permission of Times Books, a division of Quadrangle/The New York Times Book Co., Inc.

From *Canajan, Eh?* by Mark M. Orkin. Copyright 1973 by Mark M. Orkin. Used by permission of General Publishing Co. Limited, 30 Lesmill Road, Don Mills, Ontario.

*American Dialects: A Manual for Actors, Directors, and Writers* by Lewis and Marguerite Shalett Herman. Copyright 1947 by Lewis and Marguerite Shalett Herman, renewed 1974. Used with permission of the publishers, Theatre Arts Books, 153 Waverly Place, New York, N.Y.

From *The Grapes of Wrath* by John Steinbeck. Copyright 1939, renewed 1967 by John Steinbeck. Reprinted by permission of Viking Penguin Inc.

Library of Congress Cataloging in Publication Data

Espy, Willard R
Say it my way.

1. English language—Pronunciation.  2. English language—Spoken English.  I. Title.
PE1137.E85    421'.54

ISBN: 0-385-13101-1
Library of Congress Catalog Card Number 79–7218
Copyright © 1980 by Willard R. Espy
All Rights Reserved
Printed in the United States of America
First Edition

To
my five children

Mona Margaret
Freddy Medora
Joanna Page
Cassin Richardson
Jefferson Taylor

who say it *their* way—and very well, too

# THANK YOU

For typing: in New York, Mary A. Klein; in Oysterville, Helen Brown. For haircuts: in New York, Alma Kovisars; in or near Oysterville, Kristine Leback. For help on vocabulary: in New York, Chig Kugel; in or near Oysterville, Joan Sonntag. For references: in New York, the New York Society Library; in or near Oysterville, the Timberland Library, and especially Mrs. Clyde Sayce. For making Xerox copies, and smiling occasionally at the verses: in New York, Jane Townsend and Dan Mosera. For everything: in New York, Louise; in Oysterville, Louise.

# CONTENTS

*A Word for Openers*                                                    xi

1. *"E Pluribus Unum,"* said the Hermit Hoar                            1

2. The hodgepodge of the Hermit Hoar                                   11

3. The Hermit Hoar on regional dialects                                27

4. Ethnic                                                              41
   P.S. Between Two Loves.

5. Idioms, colloquia, and a few toots                                  57
   Get. All. Caboodle. Fishing. Baseball. Words and
   music.

6. Slang, fads, and counter-culture                                    65
   CB lingo. Women's lib. Cockney rhyming slang. Cow-
   boy slang. Laid back. Black English and the counter-
   culture.

7. Error, confusion, and jargon                                        79
   Malapropisms. Homonyms. Jargon.

8. Sesquipedalia                                                       89
   Long words. Double-dactyls. Sesquipedalian limericks.
   Words with one syllable.

9. Pronunciation, with ½ tbsp. spelling            95
Shibboleth. *Cicero ce-ci*. Lollapaloosa. Acceptable pronunciation. Lazy pronunciation. Spelling. Words often
mispronounced.

10. Vocabulary                                     107
Optimum size. Precision. *Punch* version. Verses to improve your vocabulary.

11. Usage                                          151
Canute. Rules frequently ignored. Exit rigidity. Logic
in grammar. Tenses. Syntax. Syllepsis.

*Afterword*                                        163

*Verses on Pronunciation*                          167

*Verses on Usage*                                  185

*Appendix I:* Pronunciation Review                 202

*Appendix II:* Correct Definitions                 204

*First Lines of Espy Verses*                       215

*First Lines of Verses by Other Authors*           218

# A WORD FOR OPENERS

This book is intended to help you in everyday speech. If your desire is to *write* better, find another book.

Speech has roots, and the separate words of speech have roots. Stir those roots a bit, and it will astonish you how your own speech will bloom. The reasons you talk as you do go back a long way—thousands of years; your utterance is bred into you, and you know a lot more about it than you may think. A good part of the following pages will be devoted not to imparting unfamiliar facts about speech, but to pointing out knowledge you carry around so habitually that you have forgotten it is there. Repeatedly, as you read, I expect you to say, "Why, I knew that all the while!"—and so you did, but the knowledge was tucked away somewhere past the edge of your consciousness. How much fun it would be if you turned your mind once in a while to the millions of things you know without knowing you know them! A friend fails in business, and you say, "He struck out." You know perfectly where that expression comes from, but the chances are ten to one that as you utter it baseball never enters your mind. What a sandlot universe would careen past if for the brief moment it takes to say, "He struck out," you remembered games you had watched or played in—laughed at the rhubarbs of the players—saw the umpire's thumb go up, and caught his roar, "I calls 'em the way I sees 'em!"

So I propose to tell you something about how language itself grew, and then how your personal language may have become what it is. Once that knowledge is part of your consciousness, I am sure you will find the world of speech a circus ring of excitement as long as you live.

Language, or at least communication, did not begin with writing, speech, or even sound. It existed before animals had evolved far enough to vocalize, or insects to stridulate. It was carried out through such media as wriggles, swellings, shrinkings, advances, retreats, and stenches. Later animals added the moos, bleats, quacks, barks, growls, howls, hisses, chirps, and the like, that are the spoken language of the beasts; what they are communicating is sometimes clear, but often a mystery. Homo sapiens gradually refined the meanings of the sounds he uttered. He scratched pictures of mastodons on cave walls, and writing began; the grunt that meant mastodon was transferred to the drawing.

Most human communication still does not start with the written, or even the spoken, word. It begins with a look, a gesture, a blow, a puff on a peace pipe. Speech comes next. For clarity, it has been forced to borrow some of the rules of writing; but it is a different animal. In the words of Laurence Urdang, editor of *Verbatim:* "Speech must differ from writing in several important ways. Sound is fleeting; the message must get through the first time or be repeated. In order to get through the first time, it must be presented in a palatable form, not riddled with arcane sesquipedalianisms or convoluted by recondite syntax.* It cannot be too concentrated or condensed. Speech must be punctuated by redundancy . . ."

Part of the art of speech, too, is listening. No matter how well you talk, your conversation is a failure if you ignore what the other person says.

When sound is added to sense, as in poetry and music, words burst into new bloom. The secret of great prose style is the sound, echoing in the back of the reader's mind. Clarity is a virtue; but sound and association fix overtones of emotion and grace into the written word as a hurricane drives straws into a wall.

I shall have failed if you finish this book talking as if you were writing an essay.† The point is to make words your friends, your companions, and something closer than either. This requires emphasizing the distinction between the spoken and the written word, while acknowledging their ultimate interdependence.

* Wow!
† That is the way the Hermit Hoar and I talk in the following pages, to be sure. But ours isn't talk; it's an essay in quotation marks.

There is no guarantee that this book will make you a charming conversationalist, the magnet of any party. Nor would I promise even that you will speak with complete correctness. In the first place, correctness is a matter of opinion. In the second place, no small part of the charm of informal speech is that it is something other than an oral version of writing. Were we to insist in speech on absolute accuracy of syntax, or even of word meanings, we might as well keep our mouths shut and exchange written notes. But I do promise to make your conversation more enjoyable for you and for others as well.

Talk, then, not writing, is the theme of this book. I pay no attention to punctuation, which is only the way we indicate on the written page the various pauses, emphases, and arrangements of words that are automatic in speech. Similarly, I make but the most cursory of bows to spelling. As far as I am concerned, you are doing fine if you can spell well enough to look up a word in your dictionary. (I know a man who was frustrated for years because he could never find the definition of *minuscule;* he thought it was *miniscule.*)

* * *

When David Brown, co-producer of *Jaws,* began talking at lunch one day about the great gap that stretched between the written and the spoken language, my first response was that he was no speech expert; he could not even teach that shark of his to talk. But after donkeys' years in Hollywood, a speech expert is exactly what Mr. Brown is.

"The trouble with writing about talking," he said, "is that it is so easy to assume that talking is just writing out loud. No such thing. John O'Hara, the novelist, had as sharp a sense of dialogue as any man who ever typed with two fingers. But when he first came to Hollywood, his dialogue didn't 'play.' He had written it for reading, not speaking. It was sharp, natural, illuminating; the *mot* was always *juste.* But the language was ocular, not oral.

"In normal conversation, the way we two are talking right now" (I was not saying a word), "everything goes in hops and jumps. We gee and haw and back up. We talk with our feet and our hands and a twitch of our eyebrows. We shout. We whisper. We swear. We giggle. We rub our eyes and noses. Our minds fill in missing words, and ignore extraneous ones—we know they are only fillers, taking up time while whoever is talking tries to remember a name or catch someone's eye across the room. When you say 'hello,' I may know you mean 'good-by.' If a man and a woman are discussing stock options over coffee, the real talking may be going on between the man's left hand and the woman's right hand, or the other way around, hidden under the table."

(The foregoing remarks are a written version of what Mr. Brown told me. He was acting out most of the conventions he mentioned, except that his hands were above the table.)

"You worship words," he said, "as I do. And we both know that the best way to worship them is to keep them in their place. President Andrew Jackson once said that a man who knew only one way to spell a word could not be very smart. By the way, when Harvard presented him with an LL.D. in 1833, Jackson had a small problem. His schooling was meager, and the address was in Latin. To express his thanks, Jackson thundered out all the Latin he knew: *'E pluribus unum,* my dear friends! *Sine qua non! Multum in parvo! Quid pro quo! Ne plus ultra!'* "

Brown and Jackson are right. Respect words; love them and, if they permit, make love to them; but never let them henpeck you. Not to worry if, as you proceed through the pages ahead, your conversation begins to sound worse to you, not better. You will have attained the level of the author who complained to a critic, "I have written ten books, and each grows worse than the one before." "Not at all," rejoined the critic; "it is simply that your taste is improving."

One good thing about words is that they are not jealous. The more of them you fall in love with, the better they like it. But they are unpredictable. An old-shoe word that has been scuffing around all your life may suddenly spread angels' wings and soar off, singing hosannas.

Propose to the language, marry, and see what happens. I hope you will emerge from this book afizz in head and heart. Aglow. Fresh from a verbal honeymoon.

# AUTHOR'S NOTE

Verses on pronunciation, vocabulary, and usage appear at frequent intervals in this book. They are not meant to be read systematically. Cumulatively, though, they should increase your pleasure and assurance in spoken English.

Unless otherwise noted, verses are by me.

## ON THE SEVENTH DAY GOD RESTED

In the beginning was the Word,
   Still slightly ungrammatical;
God taught six days, but then occurred
   The seventh, a sabbatical.
He rang the bell next day, no doubt,
But all his pupils had dropped out.

# SAY IT MY WAY

# ONE

## "E PLURIBUS UNUM,"
## SAID THE HERMIT HOAR

Start with the relationship between my great-uncle Allie, better
known as Mr. Anonymous, and the Hermit Hoar.

The Hermit Hoar was first called to public attention in the eighteenth century by Dr. Samuel Johnson, panjandrum of lexicogra-
phers, through the following poem:

Hermit hoar, in solemn cell
  Wearing out life's evening grey;
Strike thy bosom, Sage, and tell
  What is bliss, and which the way.

Thus I spoke, and speaking sigh'd,
  Scarce repress'd the starting tear,
When the hoary sage reply'd,
  Come, my lad, and drink some beer.

Uncle Allie, who met the Hermit Hoar in 1880 through the British poet William Brighty Rands, considered the last line of Johnson's verse a revolutionary insight, comparable to Newton's discovery of the law of gravitation. The only passage that compared
with it in English, he asserted, was A. E. Housman's "Malt does
more than Milton can/To justify God's ways to man."* The sage

* There are those who insist that in 1880 A. E. Housman had not yet written
"Malt does more than Milton can . . ." I tell the tale as it was told.

and Mr. Anonymous, of one mind as to what is bliss, and which the way, became firm friends, and merry companions. In the 1930s, when Mr. Anonymous retired to my home village—Oysterville, Washington—the Hermit Hoar followed him, setting up a solemn cell in the swamps between the hamlet and the ocean. Here the two men forgathered almost nightly, generally under the chaperonage of Author Unknown, the gigantic mongrel dog that attended Mr. Anonymous wherever he went. It must have puzzled the skunks, bears, garter snakes, and other beasts in the neighborhood of the solemn cell to hear two aged but powerful voices, accompanied by the howling of a dog, raised through the night in song; the refrain was always, "Come, my lad, and drink some beer."

Uncle Allie—you will have to forgive my slipping back and forth between my two names for him—died peacefully in 1976, at the age of 116. I have since been using his cottage as a retreat. By undeserved good fortune I have been accepted by the Hermit Hoar as a substitute, watered down, for my uncle.

It was natural, therefore, that I should turn for counsel to the Hermit Hoar when I undertook to write this book on the spoken word; after all, the Hermit Hoar was the discovery of Samuel Johnson, the greatest lexicographer of them all. So on an evening last winter when the rain was scudding evilly from the southeast, and the teeth of the windows in my cottage were a-chatter, I donned my heavy-weather gear and tramped off to the solemn cell for a conference. Author Unknown, who has never treated me with the devotion he accorded my uncle, remained at home, nose within his paws by the subsiding fire.

The solemn cell in which the Hermit Hoar continues to wear out life's evening grey (what a long twilight it must be for him!) consists of a cabin of unsplit alder logs, with mud daubed between them to inhibit the wind. The cabin measures, at a guess, fifteen by twenty feet. A kerosene lamp, suspended from the ceiling, burns day and night; it has to be perpetual because the two windows, facing each other in the middle of the side walls, are never washed or opened. The floor is an irregular agglomeration of logs split out of the driftwood cast up by the Pacific Ocean, a half mile to the west. When the Hermit Hoar and I pause in our conversation, which is seldom, we can hear the beat of the ocean breakers, like the distant rush of automobiles on an expressway. Spruce or alder logs blaze day and night in a fireplace at the back of the cell. At one side of the fireplace is the camp cot which serves the Hermit Hoar as bed. At the other are two aged rocking chairs. The Hermit Hoar, thin-blooded these days, sits in the one nearest the fire, basking in the warmth. I have a third chair, an affair cobbled together from two-by-fours. It does not rock.

A curious feature of the solemn cell is a windlass at its center.

From this depend two eighth-of-an-inch ropes that disappear into a hole, or well, in the floor. The Hermit Hoar insists that by turning the crank at the south end of the windlass, he can produce the sweetest water to be found in Oysterville. I have never seen this crank used. The crank at the north end, turned at a deliberate pace, brings from the bowels of the earth a dripping earthenware jug of icy draft beer. Why the jug remains forever full is a mystery. I have no idea where the beer originates, nor do I consider it my business to ask.

As I doffed my dripping sou'wester and slicker, I offered my customary salutation:

Strike thy bosom, Sage, and tell
What is bliss, and which the way.

The Hermit Hoar—a thin, stooped old man, with sharp blue eyes, a relief-map of wrinkles on his clean-shaven face, and a head bald save for a fringe of white hair around the ears—replied ritually, as he decanted from the jug into two stoneware mugs:

Come, my lad, and drink some beer.

He handed me my mug, and blew the barm from his. (The Hermit Hoar refers to the head on his beer as barm, but insists on my saying foam; barm, he says, is too good a word for Americans.)

"I have a problem," I said. "I have agreed to write a book on how to master spoken English in thirty days."

"You have agreed to write a book in thirty days? Off with you, lad; you must get at it."

"You misunderstand me. My book must enable any reader to master spoken English within a thirty-day period."

"I see. What is the problem?"

"Obviously, it is impossible to master the language in thirty days. I have not mastered it in twice that many years."

"But your book may help a few people to speak better, and perhaps increase their self-confidence in the process. That is nothing to be ashamed of. Let me give you Rule No. 1 for your project: Drink another beer."

"Gladly. Now, my first problem is, when did communication begin? As I walked over here the coyotes were howling. What were they saying?"

"My impression, lad, is that you are holding back part of your problem."

I said, "Perhaps I am becoming superstitious. How long ago did Uncle Allie die?"

"Three years come November."

I reached into an inner pocket of my denim jacket (an ancient, paint-spattered hand-me-down from my father), and removed two folded papers. "Every day of those three years," I said, "I have been codifying his manuscripts for inclusion in a definitive *Encyclopedia Anonymica*. I thought I had seen them all. Yet this morning, on the very top of the pile, were two sets of rhymes that were never there before, both dealing with the subject of this book."

"One moment, lad," said the Hermit Hoar, "while I fetch some beer . . . Now" (he had blown off his barm), "let me hear the verses."

"This is the first one—in Uncle Allie's own handwriting:

Be warned, when Bruin's lip retracts,
To guard your inner artifacts.
If on its tail the rattlesnake
Plays castanets, that spot forsake.

The squirrel in the white owl's beak
Affrights the dark with dying shriek.
The rabbit hanging in the snare
Bends eye reproachful on its slayer.

With oestral redolence as bait
The bug and bitch attract their mate.
Men turn to mold, and words to weeds:
Communication thus proceeds."

"It sounds authentic," said the Hermit Hoar. "Right up Allie's alley. Perhaps your uncle is starting to haunt your cottage. If you run into him, would you ask him to drop by for a beer?"

I was not amused.

"I am reminded," he went on, "that Dr. Abraham Moles—singularly appropriate name!—a researcher into animal language, has assigned meanings to the six chirps, or stridulations, of the male grasshopper. If you allot a line to each sound, you will produce this free-verse sestet" [here the Hermit Hoar's own voice became not unlike a chirp; it could scarcely have been a stridulation, since he was not rubbing his legs together]:

it is fine—life is good
i would like to make love
you are trespassing on my territory
she's mine!
o how nice it would be to make love
o how nice to have made love

"Does the rhythm have to match the chirps?" I asked. "If not, I could put it like this:"

Life is fine—to feel, to move:
Even better, to make love.
*Do not step across this line:*
  *She's mine!*
O, how nice it is to dote—
Nice too, afterwards, to gloat!

The Hermit Hoar was not listening. "Have you ever heard the mating call of a bull moose?" he asked.

I had to admit that I had not.

He cupped his hands before his mouth. There blared through the solemn cell the eeriest and loudest moan I had heard this side of a graveyard.

"Stop!" I begged. "A maiden moose may come calling!"

"It has been known to happen," said the Hermit Hoar complacently.

At about this time the thread of our conversation grew tangled. It seems to me that we spent a considerable period challenging each other to identify imitations of animal signals. We mimicked the sounds insects make by rubbing leg against leg or wing against wing; the drumming of fishes; the chest slappings of gorillas. I bested the Hermit Hoar only once, when, portraying a fiddler crab seeking to attract a mate, I scuttled around the cell, one arm aloft with the hand frantically waving. My first failure came when he jigged around the well. He would rise on tiptoe, dip to his knee, dart right, and then left.

"The dance of the honeybee," he said when I gave up. "No scientist has been able to explain how bees tell one another not only the direction of a food source but just how far away it is. For that matter, no scientist has ever been able to explain how a bumblebee is able to fly."

Having won, it was his turn again, and he emitted a series of gurgling whistles. I guessed that he was imitating a canary, but he was singing the song of the beluga whale.

The game slowed to a stop, like a swing when the old cat dies. I was drowsing. The Hermit Hoar seemed to speak from far away when he said, "To business. We have demonstrated that communication exists among even the lowest animals. What is the next step?"

"According to the second verse I found it is body language."

"So what is the verse?"

I took a long pull from my mug, wiped my mustache with the back of my hand, and read slowly, with careful articulation:

# WITH QUIZZIC BROW

With quizzic brow, or lashes lowered;
With glances forward, glances froward;
With lip that sneers, incisor bare;
With dreamy smile, or absent stare;
With eyes asquint, or wide with pain;
With knees uncrossed that cross again;
With hands on hips, or clasped in prayer;
With look unfixed, now here, now there;
With breath uneven; pumping wrist;
With slackened spine and flaccid fist;
With flut of finger, tap of toe . . .
We learn the facts we need to know.
A tome spills out of every look—
Yet not a word in all the book.

The Hermit Hoar pulled his ancient nose. "Flut . . . flut," he mused. "Innovative writer, your Uncle Allie. Much neater to flut than to flutter, I should think."

One of us then recited a poem by David Law Proudfit. The title was "Prehistoric Smith. Quaternary Epoch—Post-pliocene period." It went this way:

A man sat on a rock and sought
  Refreshment from his thumb;
A dinotherium wandered by
  And scared him some.

His name was Smith. The kind of rock
  He sat upon was shale.
One feature quite distinguished him—
  He had a tail.

The danger past, he fell into
  A revery austere;
While with his tail he whisked a fly
  From off his ear.

"Mankind deteriorates," he said,
  "Grows weak and incomplete;
And each new generation seems
  Yet more effete.

"Nature abhors imperfect work,
  And on it lays her ban;

And all creation must despise
   A tailless man.

"But fashion's dictates rule supreme,
   Ignoring common sense;
And fashion says, to dock your tail
   Is just immense.

"And children now come in the world
   With half a tail or less;
Too stumpy to convey a thought,
   And meaningless.

"It kills expression. How can one
   Set forth, in words that drag,
The best emotions of the soul,
   Without a wag?"

Sadly he mused upon the world,
   Its follies and its woes;
Then wiped the moisture from his eyes,
   And blew his nose.

But clothed in earrings, Mrs. Smith
   Came wandering down the dale;
And, smiling, Mr. Smith arose,
   And wagged his tail.


"Well wagged," said the Hermit Hoar. (It must have been I who recited the verse.) "But surely you are not going to devote an entire book about spoken English to speech without words, are you?"

"Not at all. These evolutionary matters are only preliminary. The balance of the book will deal with the usual conventions: pronunciation, vocabulary, usage."

A despondent note entered the voice of the Hermit Hoar. He said, "My lad, you take this book seriously, don't you?"

"Of course I do."

"Would you take advice from one old enough to be your father?"

Father? The Hermit Hoar was old enough to be my great-great-great . . . I tried dizzily to count the greats.

But I managed to nod.

"Don't take yourself too seriously, lad. After your book comes out, the over-all quality of conversation will remain much as it has always been. To use an Americanism, it will still be lousy."

"Now jusht a minute!" I protested. (It was becoming difficult to shape my tongue around my words.) "Anybody who follows my shuggeshtionsh can't help shpeaking better English."

"But how many will really follow your suggestions? How many will stick it out? One out of ten? Twenty? None at all? Real improvement will require a regular schedule of hard work. It will require persistence. And persistence requires motivation. The men and women who buy self-help books—make no bones about it, lad, yours will be a self-help book, no matter how you disguise it—are precisely the part of our population with the least motivation. They are the ones who are always looking for miracle cures."

"Makesh no differensh," I said with dignity. "Even if they don't learn anything, they'll enjoy themselves."

"Yes, there is always that," said the Hermit Hoar . . .

* * *

*"E pluribus unum!"* the Hermit Hoar was shouting into my ear.

"Eh? Eve pluried what?" I mumbled, trying not to come awake.

"The motto of your country, lad! *Your* country! The land of the free and the brave! The shrine of each patriot's devotion!"

"Thought it wazh 'In God we trust.' "

"Look at the other side of your coins. *'E pluribus unum'!* One out of many!"

I was still rubbing my eyes.

"Not just one people out of many—one language out of many! The theme of your book! Come, my lad—let us drink to Latin!"

We drank to Latin.

"Let us drink to Greek!"

We drank to Greek.

"Let us drink to Celtic!"

"To Anglo and Saxon!"

We drank. We also drank to Danish and Norman French. We then turned to the modern languages, including Swahili and Mandarin Chinese. When my head slumped again, the Hermit Hoar was still happily calling out toasts. When I woke, he had reached his own native country. He had also established a rhythm. The jug that never ran dry was clutched in his left hand; the mug was in his right. He would loft the mug and shout, "To the dialect of Northumberland!" Then he would blow the barm in the direction of the well, drain the mug, refill it, and repeat the process:

"To the dialect of Tyne and Wear! . . . Of Durham! . . . Of Cumbria! . . . Of North Yorkshire! . . . Of West Yorkshire! . . . Of Lancashire! . . . Manchester! . . . Merseyside! . . . Chester! . . . Derby! . . . South York! . . . Humberside Hull! . . . Gwynedd! . . . Clwyd! . . . Salop! . . . Stafford! . . . Nottingham! . . . Lincoln! . . . Dyfed! . . . Powys! . . . Hereford and Worcester! . . . Warwick! . . . Leicester! . . . Northampton! . . . Cambridge! . . . Norfolk! . . . Suffolk! . . . Essex! . . . Hertford! . . . Bedford! . . .

Bucks! . . . Oxford! . . . Gloucester! . . . Gwent! . . . West Glamorgan! . . . Bristol! . . . Somerset! . . . Wiltshire! . . . Berkshire! . . . London! . . . Surrey! . . . East Sussex! . . . West Sussex! . . . Hampshire! . . . The Isle of Wight! . . . Dorset! . . . Devon! . . . Cornwall!"

"You forgot Kent," I said.

"To the dialect of Kent!" he toasted. "My lad, the wonder of it! One standard English language of such mongrel antecedents! Why, even the regional accents and locutions of your own great country are all the offspring of the dialects of the first British colonists!"

The solemn cell was revolving slowly in a clockwise direction. I said very clearly, "Wizh an admishture from the Inzhuns who met 'em when they landed, the blacksh they imported as shlaves, the buzhinessmen they traded wizh on shea voyagezh. Wizh Frenshmen to the north and Shpanairdsh to the shouth. And wizh sheveral million immigrants who followed along behind."

"Well put," said the Hermit Hoar. "I am sure your book will cover them all in due course. Which is why you must never insist, lad, on turning spoken English into a wad of homogeneous dough. It is natural for a Texan to bawl like a calf. It is also natural"—here he fixed me with a glittering eye—"for a drunk to talk like a drunk."

He was beginning to revolve with the solemn cell.

"One last warning," he said. "Eschew all jargon, and all words like 'eschew.'"

"I 'gree. I'll tell 'em zhey can shay anyshing any way zhey want to. Long azh zhey shay it my way."

A deep, commanding bark sounded outside the door.

Author Unknown had come to fetch me home.

# TWO

## THE HODGEPODGE
## OF THE HERMIT HOAR

"FROM time to time," said the Hermit Hoar, turning his wind-lass, "pilgrims come to me and ask, 'Hermit Hoar in solemn cell, who are you?'"

I know a hint when I hear one.

"Hermit Hoar, who are you?" I asked.

He waggled his forefinger at my nose and recited solemnly,

Oh, I am a cook, and a captain bold,
And the mate of the *Nancy* brig,
And a bo'sun tight, and a midshipmite,
And the crew of the captain's gig.

"Oh, you mean you are W. S. Gilbert," I said.

"I mean, as you well know, lad, that there flows in me, as in you, the blood of ten thousand warring tribes. Britain has been inhabited for at least fifty thousand years. Until the time of the Romans, and then of William, it must have been overrun at least once a year, if not once a season, by marauders from the Continent. It stands to reason that the first settlers were Paleolithics, and that Neolithics succeeded them."

"Uncle Allie," I said, "once told me that he could write down our family genealogy in five lines. And he did, too. They went:

A Neolith of the name of Smith
Took over the cave of a Paleolith.
  He was much admired
  As he ceaselessly sired
All our Paleo-Neolo kin and kith."


"To proceed," said the Hermit Hoar. "The Neolithics turned somehow into the swarthy little fellows who were the first Scottish Picts. They may have sprung from an early Mediterranean race. Then the ancient Celts arrived in two separate batches, speaking the language that grew into present-day Gaelic and Welsh. They ruled the islands until the Romans took over in the first century A.D."

"I once read," I said, "that when the Romans abandoned Britain in 410, they left an army of gigantic Nubians guarding Hadrian's Wall to protect Roman Britain from the tribes of the north. If that is so, anybody whose forebears go back to early England must have a touch of African blood."

"That is as may be," said the Hermit Hoar, handing me a beer. (The sun had not yet set, and we were both still quite sober; so I think my memory of his remarks is accurate.) "But our subject is language, not race. The Romans ruled Britain for over three hundred years, and by the time of their departure all educated Britons were speaking Latin. In the fifth and sixth centuries, though, the island was overrun by the Anglo-Saxons, who spoke a Germanic dialect, and Latin was forgotten until William overcame the English at Hastings in 1066. French, the language of the conquerors, and Latin, the language of the church and the law, then gradually merged with the native tongue to become the English we know today."

\*    \*    \*

At this point he lost my attention; my mind had run aground on Latin, while his was rowing down the stream of time, pointing out later developments in the language. Latin, I reflected, is not tossed about much in conversation these days. Still, if you can remember a few phrases, why not show them off? You need not know what they mean; no one else will, either. Your friends may call you pretentious, but that will be only to hide their envy.

The result of my reflections was the verses that follow, though in fact I did not write them until several days after this conversation with the Hermit Hoar. The first verse is a test. I submit that even if you do not know a word of formal Latin you will have an excellent notion of how the young lady participating in the dialogue is responding to her wooer. To see whether I am right, simply scribble into the blank spaces in the second version of the verse the direction you think her replies are taking. The third version slightly alters one or two English lines for the sake of the rhyme, and provides a loose English-language approximation of the Latin.

## ROMAN COURTSHIP (*Latin included*)

I prayed, "One kiss, O fairest of thy sex!"
She breathed, *"De minimis non curat lex."*
"One kiss," I begged, "that may lead on to twenty!"
Said she: *"Ad arbitrium, Deo volente."*
"Yet, love may bruise; for rigorous its cult is!"
She said, *"Experienta docet stultos."*
"Dare I aspire so high, dear doe, dear lady?"
A fleeting smile. Quoth she, *"Experto crede."*
"Will love, then, blaze on us in all its glory?"
*"Omnis vincit amor, nos et cedamis amori."*
"Your eyes seem melting. Can this truly be?"
*"Flamma a fumo est proxima,"* said she.
"But should I shame thee . . . harm thee . . . I would die!"
*"Volenti non fit injuria,"* came her sigh.
I moaned, "Thou'lt fob me off with some excuse."
*"Adsum. Age quo agis,* silly goose!"

## ROMAN COURTSHIP (*Latin omitted*)

I prayed, "One kiss, O fairest of thy sex!"
She breathed, "_____."
"One kiss," I begged, "that may lead on to twenty!"
Said she: "_____."
"Yet, love may bruise; for rigorous its cult is!"
She said, "_____."
"Dare I aspire so high, dear doe, dear lady?"
A fleeting smile. Quoth she, "_____."
"Will love, then, blaze on us in all its glory?"
"_____."
"Your eyes seem melting. Can this truly be?"
"_____," said she.
"But should I shame thee . . . harm thee . . . I would die!"
"_____," came her sigh.
I moaned, "Thou'lt fob me off with some excuse."
"_____, silly goose!"

## ROMAN COURTSHIP (*Latin translated*)

I prayed, "Oh, fairest of thy sex, one kiss!"
She breathed, "No law bars sin so slight as this."
"One kiss," I begged, "that may lead on to twenty!"
"God helping," said she, "make the kisses plenty."
"Yet, love is rigorous. How bear its bruises?"
She said, "With practice, one learns helpful ruses."
"Dare I aspire so high, dear doe of does?"
She said, "Accept the word of one who knows."
"Will love, then, blaze on us in all its splendor?"
"Love conquers all—we may as well surrender."
"Your eyes seem melting. Is it with desire?"
"It's fair to guess that where there's smoke there's fire."
"But should I shame thee—harm thee—I would die!"
"The willing feel no hurt," was her reply.
I moaned, "Thou'lt fob me off with some excuse."
"I'm here. Perform thy function, silly goose!"

The second verse that germinated in my mind when I should have been listening to the Hermit Hoar had to do with Latin abbreviations, so commonly used in English that we take them for granted. For instance:

## Q.E.D.

Dear wife, dear brother, sister, pal,
    *Et al.:*
For you I now jot down a squib
    (*Ad lib.*)
Of thoughts at waking. I convey 'em
    In the *A.M.,*
While you're to sort and referee 'em
    In the *P.M.*
They're very clever thoughts (*i.e.,*
    To me):
Of cabbages and kings a peck,
    *Et seq.*

Just ask me any question. *Viz.:*
· Whose woes are greater—hers, or his?
· When man and maid become one stem,
  Is it forever, or *pro tem.?*
· Which blessing in the end is better: a
  Wish denied or filled? *Etc.*

You grant my wisdom? *Q.E.D.*
Your health is poorly? *R.I.P.*

The unabbreviated Latin, with English translations, of the above abbreviations:
    · *Et al. Et alii,* "and others."
    · *Ad lib. Ad libitum,* "at pleasure."
    · *A.M. Ante meridiem,* "before noon."
    · *P.M. Post meridiem,* "after noon."
    · *I.e. Id est,* "that is."
    · *Et seq. Et sequentes,* "and the following."
    · *Viz. Videlicet,* "it is easy to see." To wit: namely.
    · *Pro tem. Pro tempore,* "for the time being."
    · *Etc. Et cetera,* "and so forth."
    · *Q.E.D. Quod erat demonstrandum,* "which was to be demonstrated."
    · *R.I.P. Requiescat in pace,* "may he [or she] rest in peace."

\* \* \*

The Hermit Hoar, noting that I was not listening, had stopped talking; but as soon as he saw that I had roused from my reverie, he continued as if there had been no pause:

"Anglo-Saxon provided the skeletal structure of modern English. The Norse and Danish Vikings invaded in the eighth and ninth centuries, and gave us such words as they, them, and their. The Norman French did the fleshing out after William's conquest."

"I suppose you were in your solemn cell all this time?"

"Not to say I wasn't," replied the Hermit Hoar, "but I am quoting most of my statistics from a book by Mario Pei called *The Story of the English Language*. Did you happen to know Pei?"

I said, "I would have liked to know him better. Mario could never refuse anyone a favor; if I telephoned him at one in the morning, he would cheerfully spend an hour helping me to render a silly macaronic verse into clear English."

"A great man," said the Hermit Hoar. "He once made the remark, obvious enough by hindsight, that the English we speak is the sum total of a long series of historical accidents. If the Romanized Britons had been able to beat back Hengist and Horsa,* English might be a Romance language today. If the Moslems had whipped Charlemagne, we might be speaking bastardized Arabic. If Harold had ducked the Norman arrows at Hastings, we might speak much like the Dutch or Germans."

"Yet even today," I said, "a man from Birmingham may be hard put to understand a man from Yorkshire."

"Yes," he said. "Despite the wireless, the telly, and the daily newspapers. Local dialects in the United States diverge little by comparison with those in England. Every dialect maintains a nodding acquaintance with standard English. You Americans always ape the winners. When George I said EYEther instead of EEther, so did the colonists in America. Americans are snobs; they opt for what they consider class. Your Pilgrims lived over ten years in Holland, yet they managed to avoid contaminating their speech with so much as one Dutch word or locution."

The Hermit Hoar was wrong on that snobbishness bit; the comparative homogeneity of the American tongue is probably due much more to two hundred years of pioneering, when one's nearest neighbor might with equal likelihood come from Maine, Virginia, Louisiana, Pennsylvania, or New York. But I hear out his opinions respectfully; both his mind and his English are generally up to date. To be sure, he pronounces news "noos," as Shakespeare did (and as news commentators on the air are doing again today). He also pronounces the noun wind "wīnd," as it was pronounced by Shakespeare in

Blow, blow thou
　Winter wīnd.
Thou art not so unkind
　As man's ingratitude.

* Hengist and Horsa were the semi-legendary leaders of the Jutes who landed in England at Ebbsfleet, Kent, in 449.

The Hermit Hoar says "obleege" for oblige, a hang-over from the eighteenth century. From the nineteenth, he says "pam" for palm and "cam" for calm, as in "the pam of your hand" and "the cam of the evening." He pronounces "preferment" as did the Vicar of Bray:

In good King Charles's golden days,
　When loyalty no harm meant,
A zealous High Churchman was I,
　And so I got prefarment.

He calls willing "wealing," as in Richard Sheridan's protest to his importunate lady loves:

I laughingly replied, " 'Tis tyrannical dealing
To make a man swear, when 'tis plain he's not
　　wealing."

"The pronunciations and the locutions of the ignorant," continued the Hermit Hoar, "are frequently amusing and even provocative. In rural England of the early nineteenth century, Thomas Hardy's characters called creatures 'craters,' child 'chiel,' empty 'empt,' undressed 'undrayed,' foot 'voot,' real 'rale,' saw 'zeed,' join 'jine,' generally 'zhinerally,' generous 'jinerous,' had 'het,' thought 'thoughted,' mischief 'mischty,' sat 'zot,' would 'woot,' chamber 'chammer,' daughter 'da'ter.' A few such locutions may work their way into general English. Most, however, die out, or remain in their little enclaves, and the language goes on according to the tastes of the powerful and the wealthy. Snobbery wins in the end."

"I hate to say this, hoary sage," I said, "but perhaps you are falling behind the times. There is a very articulate school, including many professional linguists, that insists that whatever is, is right." I adduced in evidence a letter to the editor of the New York *Times*:

> Ordinary language is as rich in metaphor, neologism, experimental syntax, peculiar diction, and in some cases rhyme and meter, as is literary language, and like that form of language it is in a constant state of flux: new forms and new words are continually being tried out, old ones discarded.

"Of course, of course," said the Hermit Hoar. "What the man does not realize is that the decisions are going to be made in the end not by the bottom, but by the top. Many may propose, and many may agree, but it is the few who dispose. Otherwise the language would become babble. New locutions sprout, like jewels from the goosegirl's tongue. But it is the responsibility of the literate, who know the basic laws of metaphor, syntax, diction, rhyme, and meter, to separate the gold from the dross. Nonstandard English does not become standard simply by emerging; it becomes standard by justifying its existence. Thousands of slang phrases have entered the mainstream of English; other thousands have endured over the centuries, yet remain as unmistakably slang today as when they were first conceived on the wrong side of the blanket.

"I can pull from my head a hundred examples of dialects that never aspired to leave their native counties. Take this from George Eliot's *Adam Bede:* 'Ay, sure; but wunna ye come in, Adam? Miss Mary's i' th' house, and Mester Burg 'ull be back anon; he'd be glad to have supper wi'm, I'll be's warrand.' The speaker was saying what came naturally; he was not pressing his version of English on the outside world. Do you remember Sam Small, Eric Knight's flying Yorkshireman? He said to his wife, 'Them? Eigh, Mully, they're nowt but a lot o' mawngy owd toffs—sitting on the park benches each day waiting for t'undertakker to come along and measure 'em. Ah can't mak friends wi' the like o' yon. Why, they got such a bloody funny accent† Ah gate nobbut one word i' ten o' what they're yammering abaht.' But Sam had no idea of forcing his locutions on Americans. My complaint about the present generation of people old and young, who go around making remarks like 'Like wow, man, I'm laid back,' is not that the code is suitable at best for adolescents, but that the speakers, though they are not sure of exactly what they mean, are convinced that they are adding new depths and insights to the spoken language, and sneer at anyone who disagrees.

"I object, too," continued the Hermit Hoar, "to writers who claim to render flawlessly pronunciations and usages that vanished hundreds of years back. They may have records of how the speech was copied on paper at the time, but how do they know what it sounded like? Were they there listening? Were there cassettes and tapes to preserve the accents? Well, I *was* there"—here he hesitated, for he was not about to give away his age—"and if I had a mind to, I could tell you just how wrong some of those reconstructions are.

"R. D. Blackmore wrote in the nineteenth century. Now it is perfectly true that rural English dialects change slowly; but Blackmore could not possibly be sure that a farm woman spoke like this one from his romance *Lorna Doone,* which is laid in the seventeenth century" (he pursed his lips, and the voice of a crone issued from his mouth):

"'Men is desaving, and so is galanies; but the most desaving of

† He was referring to the senior citizens—many of them on the verge of becoming graduate citizens—who may be found sitting on Los Angeles park benches.

all is books, with their heads and tails, and speckots in 'em, lik a peg as have taken the maisles.' "

"I love it, I love it! What was she saying?"

" 'Desaving' is 'deceiving'; 'galanies' is from the French for 'chicken'; 'speckots' is 'specks'; 'peg' is 'pig'; and 'maisles' is 'measles'. She was saying that men and chickens are both deceiving, but that books are the most deceiving of all, with their silly-looking letters pretending to mean something. John Ridd, her master, explains her better than I can: 'It was part of Betty's obstinacy,' he writes, 'that she never would believe in reading, or the possibility of it, but stoutly maintained to the very last, that people first learned things by heart, and then pretended to make them out from patterns done upon paper, for the sake of astonishing honest folk, just as do the conjurors.' "

\* \* \*

British pronounciations and dialects still bemuse Americans. A few examples:

The town of Salisbury was once called Sarum. The abbreviated form of Hampshire is Hants. Hence the celebrated limerick:

## THE YOUNG CURATE OF SALISBURY

There was a young curate of Salisbury
Whose manners were quite halisbury-skalisbury.
   He ran around Hampshire
   Without any pampshire,
Till the vicar compelled him to walisbury.

—Anonymous

Here Salisbury is pronounced "Sarum," forcing halisbury-skalisbury to become "harum-scarum," and walisbury "wear 'em." Pronouncing Hampshire as Hants forces pampshire into "pants."

The names Cholmondeley and Colquhoun are pronounced Chumley and Coon, giving us:

## A YOUNG MAN CALLED CHOLMONDELEY COLQUHOUN

A young man called Cholmondeley Colquhoun
Kept as a pet a babolquhoun.
   His mother said, "Cholmondeley,
   Do you think it quite colmondeley
To feed your babolquhoun with a spolquhoun?"

—Anonymous

*Some English place names:*

| THE NAME | THE WAY THEY SAY IT |
|---|---|
| Abergavenny | aber-genny |
| Leominster | lem-ster |
| Cirencester | sis-e-ter |
| Churchtown | chow-zen |
| Uttoxeter | uck-ster |
| Godmanchester | gum-sister or gon-shister |
| Wymondham | win-dum |
| Jervaulx | jar-vis |
| Amotherby | amer-by |
| Pontrefact | pom-fret |
| Lympne | lim |
| Mousehole | moo-zel |
| Ulgham | uff-am |
| Ulverston | oo-ston |

*Some Scottish place names:*

| | |
|---|---|
| Kircudbright | ker-koo-bree |
| Balquhidder | bal-widder |
| Dalziel | dee-ell |
| Borrowstounness | bo-nes |

Erse, or Gaelic, has its own oddities of pronunciation: Cuchulain, for instance, sounds like Coolin:

The pronunciation of Erse
Gets worse and worse.
They spell it Cuchulain—
No fuchulain.

— A. D. Hope

To say 'ouse and 'orrible was in London first the sign of the snob, later of the slob, as in Mrs. Crawford's "The 'orn of the 'unter is 'eard on the 'ill," and Moore's "A 'eart that is 'umble might 'ope for it 'ere." The Cockney drops the initial aspirate, but inserts it where it does not belong:

A helephant heasily heats at his hease
Hunder humbrageous humbrella trees.

Cockney, the accent of Londoners "born within the sound of the Bow bells," emphasizes wordplay. The two verses that follow give an idea of how it sounds:

# THE POOR OLD 'ORSE

We 'ad a little outing larst Sunday arternoon;
And sech a jolly lark it was, I shan't forget it soon!
We borrered an excursion van to take us down to Kew,
And—oh, we did enjoy ourselves! I don't mind telling *you*.

> *The Chorus.*  For we 'ad to stop o' course,
> Jest to bait the bloomin' orse,
> So we'd pots of ale and porter
> (Or a drop o' something shorter),
> While he drunk his pail o' water,
> He was sech a whale on water!
> 'Ad more water than he oughter,
> More water than he oughter,
>    'Ad the old 'orse!

At Kinsington we 'alted, 'Ammersmith, and Turnham Green,
The 'orse 'ad sech a thust on him, its like was never seen!
With every 'arf a mile or so, that animal got blown:
And we was far too well brought-up to let 'im drink alone!

> *The Chorus.*  As we 'ad to stop, o' course, etc.

We stopped again at Chiswick, till at last we got to Kew,
But when we reached the Gardings—well, there was a fine to-do!
The Keeper, in his gold-laced tile, was shutting-to the gate.
Sez he, "There's no admittance now—you're just arrived too late!"

> *The Chorus.*  We've 'ad to stop, o' course, etc.

But when the van was ordered, we found—what *do* yer think?
That miserable 'orse 'ad been an' took too much to drink!
He kep' a-reeling round us, like a circus worked by steam,
An, 'stead o' keeping singular, he'd turned into a team!

> *The Chorus.*  We must wait awhile, o' course,
> Till they've sobered down the 'orse.
> Just another pot o' porter,
> Or a drop o' something shorter,
> While our good landlady's daughter
> Takes him out some soda-warter.
> For he's 'ad more than he oughter,
> He's 'ad more than he oughter,
>    'As the poor old 'orse!

So, when they brought the 'orse round, we started on our way;
'Twas 'orful 'ow the animal from side to side would sway!

Young 'Opkins took the reins, but soon in slumber he was sunk—
*When a interfering Copper run us in for being drunk!*

*The Chorus.* Why, can't yer shee? o' coursh
     Tishn't us—it ish the 'orsh!
     He's a whale at swilling water,
     We've 'ad only ale and porter,
     Or a touch o' something shorter,
     You le'mme go, you shnorter!
     Don' you tush me till you oughter!
     Jus' look 'ere—to cut it shorter—
        Take the poor old 'orsh!

(General adjournment to the police-station. The final Chorus:)

     Why, your wushup sees, o' course,
     It was all the bloomin' 'orse!
     He *would* 'ave a pail o' water
     Every 'arf a mile (or quarter),
     Which is what he didn't oughter!
     He should stick to ale or porter,
     With a drop o' something shorter,
     I'm my family's supporter—
        Fine the poor old 'orse!

         —Anonymous

## "BIBY'S" EPITAPH

A muvver was barfin' 'er biby one night
The youngest of ten and a tiny young mite.
The muvver was poor and the biby was thin,
Only a skelington covered with skin;
The muvver turned rahnd for the soap off the rack,
She was but a moment, but when she turned back,
The biby was gorn; and in anguish she cried,
"Oh, where is my biby?"—The angels replied.

"Your biby 'as fell dahn the plug-'ole,
Your biby 'as gorn dahn the plug;
The poor little thing was so skinny and thin
'E oughter been barfed in a jug;
Your biby is perfeckly 'appy,
'E won't need a barf any more,
Your biby 'as fell dahn the plug-'ole,
Not lost, but gorn before."

(I received from Mrs. J. W. Marsh of San Diego the following alternate ending to the above verse. It requires for rhyming pur-

poses a change in the fourteenth line—say to "You won't need to
barf 'im agine"):

Your biby 'as fell dahn the pluggle
Let's 'ope 'e don't stop up the dryne.

— Anonymous

Several peculiarly British locutions and pronunciations are min-
gled here:

## THE HELBATRAWSS

Qvite horfen, fer a lark, coves on a ship
   Ketches a uge sea-bird, a helbatrawss,
A hidle sod as muck in on the trip
   By follerin the wessel on its course.

Theve ardly got im on the deck afore,
   Cackanded, proper chokker—never mind
Es a igh-flier, cor, e makes 'em roar
   Voddlin abaht, is vings trailin beind.

Up top, yus, e was smashin, but es grim
   Like this: e aint alf hugly nah es dahned:
Vun perisher blows Voodbine-smoke at im,
   A number tikes im orff by oppin rahnd!

A long-aired bloke's the sime: ead in the clahds,
   E larfs at harrers, soups is cupper tea;
But dah to earf in these are bleedin crahds,
   Them uge great vings balls up his plates,
      yer see.

— Kingsley Amis

*Southern English:*

    Tom Smith, "who used to drive the Alacrity coach, would
often point to a tree near the river, from which a fine view of
the church was commanded, and inform his companion on the
box that "Artises‡ come and take hoff the Church from that
there tree.—It was a Habby once, sir."

— *Pendennis,* William Makepeace Thackeray

‡ Artists, that is.

*Scottish:*

'Twas on a Monday morning,
   Right early in the year,
That Charlie cam' to our town,
   The young Chevalier!
As he was walking up the street,
   The city for to view,
O, there he spied a bonnie lass
   The window lookin' through.

Sae light's he jimped up the stair,
   An' tirled at the pin;
An' wha sae ready as hersel
   To let the laddie in?

He set his Jenny on his knee,
   A' in his Highland dress;
For brawlie weel he kenned the way
   To please a lassie best.

                — Anonymous

*Scottish* (northeast):

    Heely, heely, Tam, ye glaiket stirk—ye hinna on the hin'
shelvin' o' the cairt. Fat hae ye been haverin' at, min? That
cauff saick'll be tintowere the back door afore we win a mile
fae hame. See't yer belly-ban be ticht aneuch noo . . .

    — *Johnny Gibb of Gushetneuk,* W. Alexander, 1871.

*The Irish of It:*

. . . I like to lie down in the sun,
   And drame when me fatures is scorchin',
That when I'm too ould for more fun,
   Why, I'll marry a wife with a fortune . . .
For I haven't a janius for work—
   It was never the gift of the Bradies—
But I'd make a most illigant Turk,
   For I'm fond of tobacco and ladies.

                — Charles Lever

*Miscellaneous:*

'Er as was 'as gone from we.
Us as is 'll go ter she.

— Traditional

On yonder hill there stands a coo,
If it's no there, it's awa noo.

— *On Yonder Hill,* William MacGonagall

With such a Babel of tongues behind them, it is hardly surprising if the accents of a Maine man and a South Carolinian do not always coincide.

# THREE

## THE HERMIT HOAR
## ON REGIONAL DIALECTS

I
N the beginning,'" I remarked, "'was the Word, and the Word
was with God, and the Word was God.'"

"John 1:1," said the Hermit Hoar. "I am glad you have picked
up a few scraps from the Bible, lad; they will do you good. The
ancient Egyptians made the same point in a different way. They
asserted that Ptah created first the other gods, then the universe,
and finally all things in it, simply by the process of uttering their
names."

"Ptah!" said I.

"You sneer," said the Hermit Hoar; "but the concept is seminal.
The difficulty is that once the gods began naming things, they
enjoyed themselves so much they could not stop. They piled words
on words; they turned old words into new ones. They are still at
it. For all the endless talk about creating a single world-wide language, we have more languages today than ever—more than 3,000,
in fact. And each influences all the rest."

It was a day dominated by one of Oysterville's rare brilliant blue
skies, across which an occasional white cloud wandered desultorily,
like a cropping cow, never bothering to raise its head. The Hermit
Hoar and I were sitting on a log in the clearing outside the solemn
cell, soaking in the unaccustomed warmth, raising our faces sky-
ward to let the sun know how welcome he was.

Our conversation was almost as desultory as the clouds, but it had a recurrent theme: the regional dialects of the United States, and their remarkable persistence in the face of the leveling influences of schools, education, radio, and television. All the dialects had started back home in Britain. England has over forty counties, and most were probably represented in the great Puritan exodus, though the East Anglican counties contributed the bulk of emigrants.

The *Mayflower* contingent originated in Scrooby, Nottinghamshire. They spoke after the fashion of southeastern England, adding a whine that some say was intended to connote piety. The Quakers, who settled Pennsylvania, brought with them the humbler dialects of northern and northwestern England. In both cases contact with their home country was at a minimum, and their speech patterns drew away from the originals.

"That was less true," said the Hermit Hoar, "among the settlers of Virginia. They clung to what they considered fashionably upper-class accents long forgotten in England. 'Jine,' they said, 'gwine,' and 'pizen,' rather than 'join,' 'going,' and 'poison'; 'varmint,' 'starling,' and '(uni)varsity,' rather than 'vermin,' 'sterling,' and 'university.' Widow became 'widder,' window 'winder,' pillow 'piller.' "

The Scotch-Irish Presbyterians who settled western Virginia and North Carolina in the eighteenth century kept linguistic ties with Scotland by sending their ministers home for religious training. "As a result," the Hermit Hoar pointed out, "they continued for generations to say 'gin' for 'if,' 'wha' for 'who,' and 'hae' for 'have.' They preserved their language heritage, too, by passing down ballads from generation to generation."

"Like 'Lord Randal,' for instance," I said.

"Yes. We must toast poor Lord Randal. Would you be a good lad, and fetch the beer?"

I obeyed with alacrity. We toasted deep, and sang. Author Unknown stirred restlessly where he was lying in the sun, and finally raised his voice in a series of intermittent howls.

"What gat ye to your dinner, Lord Randal, my son,
What gat ye' to your dinner, my handsome young man?"
"I gat eels boil'd in broo'; mother, make my bed soon,
For I'm weary wi' hunting, and fain wald lie down."

It was a lazy afternoon, and I fear we were both half asleep much of the time, but I remember most of what was said. The whole thing had started when I quoted a comment made long ago by young Ivy in John Steinbeck's *The Grapes of Wrath:*

Everybody says words different. Arkansas folks says 'em
different, and Oklahomy folks says 'em different. And we seen
a lady from Massachusetts, an' she said 'em differentest of all.
Couldn't hardly make out what she was saying.

"William Safire," I said, "once remarked that an 'oar-inge' in
California becomes an 'ar-ringe' in New England; 'grease' in New
England is 'greaze' in the South; west of the Alleghenies, the vowel
sounds in 'Mary married Harry' are indistinguishable the one from
the other, while on the Atlantic Coast Mary may turn to 'may-ree,'
'mair-ee,' or 'merry.' He also said that in Salt Lake City one praises
the 'lard' and puts the 'Lord' in the refrigerator."

"Howard K. Smith," said the Hermit Hoar—"the broadcaster
chap, you know—says the inhabitants of Baltimore call their city
'Balamer, Murlin.' They call garbage 'gobbidge,' legal 'liggle,'
clothes 'clays,' and dial—as in dialing the telephone—'doll.' 'Can-
cel' means 'council,' as in town council, while 'council' means 'can-
cel,' as a check. He once accused them of saying 'paramour' for
'power mower,' but they had him there; they said, 'What's so
strange about having a paramour to cut the grass?' "

"Speaking as a native of the state of Washington," I said, "I
know that our speech is the most nearly standard in the nation. We
Washingtonians politely mask our smiles when ignorant Easterners
pronounce the simple county name Wahkiakum as Wauky-AK-um
instead of Wau-KEYE-a-kum. We voted against John F. Kennedy
in 1960 because he made the mistake of pronouncing the town of
Spokane Spōk-ĀN instead of Spoke-ANN. Yet even we pronounce
as Squim a town name spelled S-E-Q-U-I-M. And we commonly
say 'real good,' an expression which drives the Mother Mary into
torrents of weeping when she hears it in Paradise."

The Hermit Hoar remembered (how he picks up these bits of
trivia in his solemn cell I will never know) that according to one
Jean Montgomery, a real estate dealer in the Bay area of California is called a "realator." Etcetera becomes "essetera"; in view of
"in lieu of"; and Ku Klux Klan "Ku Kluck Lan." Actually is
"acksh'lly," deteroriate "deteriate," hierarchy "high arky," respira-
tory "respitory," handle "hannel," temperature "tempature," and
aspirin "aspirn."

It seems to me that the regional accents uppermost in our minds
that afternoon were largely southern. In some cases they involved
usage as well as pronunciation. I quoted at length, for instance,
from a series of pamphlets called (in lower case) *you all spoken
here*,"* by Roy Wilder, Jr., a man with perfect pitch for southern
dialect. Here are a few of his definitions:

---

* I hope *you all spoken here* will soon appear in book form. If you cannot
find it, write to Roy Wilder, Jr., the Gourd Hollow Press, Spring Hope, North
Carolina, and he will send you copies of the manuscript. For a price, of course.

· Someone a little less than bright: "His traces ain't hooked up right" . . . "He's three pickles shy of a barrel" . . . "He's three bricks shy of a load."

· A Southerner referring to someone he knows of but does not know personally: "We've howdied but we ain't shook."

· Don't lose your temper: "Don't get cross-legged."

· An impoverished Southerner of good family: "He's too poor to paint, and too proud to whitewash."

· Violent anger: "As mad as a rooster in an empty hen-house."

· The final straw: "That takes the rag off the bush."

· To apologize publicly: "Put the spit on the apple."

· An incompetent: "A rubber-nosed woodpecker in a pet-rified forest."

According to Jim Everhart in *The Illustrated Texas Dictionary,* the language undergoes a sea-change in Texas:

· Ails. Other than the person or thing implied. "Ah only done what anybody ails would do."

· Beggar. Larger in size, height, width, amount, etc. "The beggar they come the harder they fall."

· Cheer. In this place or spot. "Yawl come riot cheer this minute."

· Fair. A distressing emotion aroused by impending danger. "The only thing we have to fair is fair itself."

· Main. Of ugly disposition, nasty. "That there is one main man."

Charleston, South Carolina, has as its lexicographer one Lord Ashley Cooper.† A small example from his dictionary of Charles-tonese:

· Abode. a wooden plank.

· Ain't. sister of one of your parents.

· Air. what you hear with, as in, "Friends, Romans, coun-trymen, lend me your airs."

· Arm. I am.

· Armageddon. I'm gonna get.

The astonishment of American English, however, is not the variety of its dialects but, to the contrary, its general uniformity. "In place of the discordant local dialects of nearly all the other countries, including England," says Mencken, "we have a general *Volkssprache* for the whole nation . . . No other country can show such linguistic solidarity."

† Pen name of Frank Gilbreth, author of *Cheaper by the Dozen* and a writer for the Charleston (S.C.) *News* and *Courier.*

By and large, therefore, our regional—as opposed to our ethnic —dialects are local curiosities, often existing happily on the same lips as general English. Some examples of local usages appear on the following pages.

*New England:*

## MIS' SMITH

All day she hurried to get through,
The same as lots of wimmin do;
Sometimes at night her husban' said,
"Ma, ain't you goin' to come to bed?"
And then she'd kinder give a hitch,
And pause half way between a stitch,
And sorter sigh, and say that she
    Was ready as she'd ever be,
        She reckoned.

And so the years went one by one,
An' somehow she was never done;
An' when the angel said as how
"Mis' Smith, it's time you rested now,"
She sorter raised her eyes to look
A second, as a stitch she took;
"All right, I'm comin' now," says she,
    "I'm ready as I'll ever be,
        I reckon."

        — Albert Bigelow Paine

*Specimens of New England Dialect:*

How be you? . . . If that ain't the beatinest! . . . I'd admire to if 'twant for the rain. . . . He like to burst his britches. . . . Shouldn't wonder but what I will. . . . Hain't a-stoppin', says I. . . . Fair gave me a conniption fit. . . . 'Twere nigh onto five mile. . . . Hit plumb snackety-dab into it. . . . Can't rightly know for sure. . . . What in tunket got you so riled up? . . . Then all at oncet she up and died.‡

‡ The dialect specimens here and in the remainder of the chapter are in most cases quoted from *American Dialects: a Manual for Actors, Director, and Writers* by Lewis and Marguerite Shalett Herman, (New York: Theatre Arts Books, 1947, fifth printing, 1973). Thank you, Hermans!

*Bronx:*

## THE BUDDING BRONX

Der spring is sprung
Der grass is riz
I wonder where dem boidies is?

Dear little boids is on der wing
Ain't dat absoid?
Der little wings is on der boid!

—Anonymous

*Brooklyn:*

## BROOKLYNESE CHAMPION

I thought the winner had been found
  The day I heard a woman make
The butcher cut her off a pound
  Of fine and juicy soylern steak.
Imagine then the dizzy whirl
  That through my head did swiftly surge
The day I heard the gifted girl
  Who wished departing friends "Bon Verge."

—Margaret Fishback

*Pittsburgh:*

Pittsburgh was once very smoky, because of the steel mills. It is now very clean. I do not know how this miracle was accomplished; perhaps they stopped making steel. Susan Cosgrove, who lives there, tells me that Pittsburghers, and indeed western Pennsylvanians generally, have developed a special way of talking. For "you" they say "you'n," using a vowel sound close to that in "Put." They do not neaten, straighten, or clean a cluttered room; they "redd it up." A dirty car "needs washed."

"Downtown" is "dahntahn" in Pittsburgh, and "northside" is "northsahd." Two-syllable words like "power" and "flour" lose a syllable, and the remaining vowel suffers a sea-change; "Howard is hired" is indistinguishable in sound from "Howard is Howard." The "l" after a vowel vanishes; "million" becomes "mi-yan." Pittsburghers also merge the sounds of hard "i" and of "ow" (as in "now") in an indescribable half-breed noise, so that (according to Michael McGough in the *Post-Gazette*) every line in the following doggerel rhymes with all the others:

Tomorrow I'll
Request a towel
To dry my owl
Beside the Nile
(And then my cow,
If I know how).

I wonder why they do not speak pure, unaccented English in
Pittsburgh, the way they do in Bahston?

*Bawlamerese:*

The Livelier Baltimore Committee has issued a guide to their
city which includes instructions on how to decipher the speech of
the natives. They explain the purpose of the guide as follows:

"We've been watching Bawlamer and its gubmint for over thirty-
five years, and we're not tarred yet! We don't work all over Merlin,
though. You won't find us in Anna Runnel, or Habberdy Grace, or
Downey Ashin, the Allanic, that is.

"We are busy, however, making sure you can get a mortgage
whether you live in Hollandtayon or Dundock. And we're concerned about how they'll dred the Patapsico. And how to get help
if your landlord won't fix a broken bawler or a leaky tawlit in your
baffroom. . . . . Whether rapid transit goes down Harrid Stret, or
across Norf Abnew, or on to the old Beeno tracks concerns us too.
And we'll call the gubmint in Naplis or Warshin to get things done.

"So while we know little of Drooslem, Arlin, or Yerp, ask us a
question about Bawlamer and we're lobble to be less ignernt. . . . ."

Some examples of Bawlamerese (As and Bs only), according to
the committee:

· Aig. The thing with a yoke.
· Arnjuice. From the sunshine tree.
· Authoritis. Arthritis.
· Arsh. People from Arlin.
· Awl. Goes into the crankcase.
· Aspern. "Take two and call me in the morning."
· Arn. What you do on an arnin board.
· Beeno. A famous railroad.
· Bleef. What you believe in.
· Bethlum. A steel mill.
· Blow. Opposite of "above."

*Hoosier:*

## LITTLE ORPHANT ANNIE

Little Orphant Annie's come to our house to stay,
An' wash the cups and saucers up, an' brush the
  crumbs away,

An' shoo the chickens off the porch, an' dust the
    hearth, an' sweep,
An' make the fire, an' bake the bread, an' earn her
    board-an'-keep;
An' all us other children, when the supper things is done,
We set around the kitchen fire and has the mostest fun
A-lis'nin' to the witch-tales 'at Annie tells about,
An' the Gobble-uns 'at gits you
        Ef you
           Don't
              Watch
                Out!

Onc't they was a little boy wouldn't say his pray'rs—
An' when he went to bed at night, away up stairs,
His mammy heard him holler, an' his daddy heard him bawl,
And when they turn't the kivvers down, he wasn't there
        at all!
An' they seeked him in the rafter-room, an' cubby-hole,
      an' press,
An' seeked him up the chimmey-flue, an' everywheres,
      I guess;
But all they ever found was thist his pants an' roundabout.
And the Gobble-uns 'll git you
        Ef you
           Don't
              Watch
                Out!

\*   \*   \*

An' little Orphant Annie says, when the blaze is blue,
An' the lampwick sputters, an' the wind goes woooo!
An' you hear the crickets quit, an' the moon is gray,
An' the lightnin' bugs in dew is all squenched away—
You better mind yer parents, and yer teachers fond and dear,
An' cherish them 'at loves you, an' dry the orphant's tear,
An' he'p the pore an' needy ones 'at clusters all about,
Er the Gobble-uns'll git you
        Ef you
           Don't
              Watch
                Out!

—James Whitcomb Riley

*California Frontier:*

# JIM

Say there! P'r'aps
Some of you chaps
   Might know Jim Wild?
Well,—no offence:
Thar ain't no sense
   In gittin' riled!

Jim was my chum
   Up on the Bar
That's why I come
   Down from up yar,
Lookin' for Jim.
Thank ye, sir! *you*
Ain't of that crew,—
   Blest if you are!

Money?—Not much;
   That ain't my kind;
I ain't no such.
   Rum?—I don't mind,
Seein' it's you.
Well, this yer Jim,
Did you know him?—
Jess 'bout your size;
Same kind of eyes;—

Well, that is strange:
   Why, it's two year
   Since he came here,
Sick, for a change.
Well, here's to us:
   Eh?
The h—— you say!
   Dead?
That little cuss?

What makes you star,
You over thar?
Can't a man drop
's glass 'n yer shop

But you must rar'?
  It wouldn't take
    D——— much to break
You and your bar.

  Dead!
Poor—little—Jim!
—Why, thar was me,
Jones, and Bob Lee,
Harry and Ben,—
No-account men:
Then to take *him!*

Well, thar—Good-bye—
No more, sir,—I—
  Eh?
What's that you say?
Why, dern it! sho!—
No? Yes! By Jo!

  Sold!
Sold! Why, you limb!
You ornery,
  Derned old
Long-legged Jim!

                —Bret Harte


*Black:*

Ralph Ellison tells me there is no one regional black dialect. At least until the great migration to the North a generation ago, the dialect changed with the region. Ellison himself was brought up in Oklahoma; his father came from one state, his mother from another. None of the three spoke the same way.

There were, however, innumerable phrases associated with blacks before city-shaped Black English received its present prominence. Among them:

I's comin'. . . . Us is both tryin'. . . . He done give it back. . . . They's somethin' funny about it. . . . My feets is tired. . . . They didn't nobody see it. . . . I was fixin' for to tell you. . . . Did I know, I'd a went. . . . He run off ever which way. . . . I like to kill him. . . . You mind (remember) where it come from? . . . They laugh they fool head off.

*Expletives:* Man . . . lordy . . . sho' nuf . . . ain't that somethin' . . . I'll be doggoned . . . dog bite me . . . dog my cats . . . ain't it the truth.

## A NEGRO LOVE SONG

Seen my lady home las' night,
  Jump back, honey, jump back.
Hel' huh han' an' sque'z it tight,
  Jump back, honey, jump back.
Hyeahd huh sigh a little sigh,
Seen a light gleam f'om huh eye,
An' a smile go flittin' by—
  Jump back, honey, jump back.

Hyeahd de win' blow thoo de pine,
  Jump back, honey, jump back.
Mockin' bird was singin' fine,
  Jump back, honey, jump back.
An' my hea't was beatin' so,
When I reached my lady's do',
Dat I couldn't ba' to go—
  Jump back, honey, jump back.

Put my ahm aroun' huh wais',
  Jump back, honey, jump back.
Raised huh lips an' took a tase,
  Jump back, honey, jump back.
Love me, honey, love me true?
Love me well ez I love you?
An' she answe'd, "Cose I do"—
  Jump back, honey, jump back.

      — Paul Laurence Dunbar

## FLY

*(As a boy, I often heard this verse recited by my cousin Jewel. I had no idea of its black derivation.)*

Po' li'l fly
Ain't got no mama,
Ain't got no papa,
Ain't got no sister,
Ain't got no brother.
No mama to love you,
No papa to love you,
No sister to love you,
No brother to love you.

Fly, I know who loves you—
God loves you.
*Go to God!*
BAM!

— Anonymous

*Some Pennsylvania Dutch Terms:*

Aint' she will? . . . Make the window shut. . . . I want
out. . . . It wonders me where he went. . . . It's going to
give a storm. . . . You're coming, ain't? . . . I mind of the
time. . . . Nice crop, say not? . . . Throw the cow over the
fence some hay. . . . He looked over the top out. . . . Leave
it stay lay. . . . He don't know what for. . . .

*Tidewater:*

We has plenty time. . . . Ah might could help you. . . .
Gotta study on it first. . . . Didn't nobody go. . . . Ain't got
no call bawling me out. . . . Don't know but what I'll take
some. . . . I got a right smart (a great deal) of work. . . .
That was powerful good. . . . It's nigh onto sundown. . . .
I'm fixin' to go out. . . . I'm going to law him in court. . . .
It was worth a sight more than I paid. . . . I'm plum beat
out. . . . He's all-fired lazy. . . . Pay her no mind. . . .

*Mountain:*

It was just a small, puny, little old thing. . . . I disremember
which was worser. . . . I'd be right proud to go. . . . He had
a power of cash money. . . . We-uns ate a heap of chickens.
. . . I don't know as I ever confidenced him. . . . Hit's a-
comin' on to rain. . . . I knowed in reason hit were his'n.
. . . Hain't never heared no such thing. . . . Whyn't yu much
me 'stead of faultin' me? . . . That 'ere buck deer'll meat us
for a spell. . . .

*Louisiana-French:*

You been try make me mad. . . . What you do now? . . .
I don't got but five cents, me. . . . He's the bestest child. . . .
He all time drink, my uncle. . . . I don't got fine clothes.
. . . I go three times. . . . I used to couldn't smoke. . . .

*Cajun:*

That man, he know the true. . . . I don't see those girl. . . .
I don't going go. . . . For why you ask me? . . . Us, we ride
two hour. . . .

*North of the Border:*

There is a family likeness between our mispronunciations in the United States and those of our neighbor to the north. In a book called *Canajan, Eh?* Mark M. Orkin cited such Canadianisms as these:

·Air. To make mistakes. "To air is yoomin, toofer give duh-vine."

·Ardic. The far north.

·Asbestos. To the extent of your ability. "You'll have ta make do asbestos you can."

·Bedder. The comparative of good.

·Berrix. Buildings where soldiers are lodged.

·Chewsday. The day after Monday.

·Dizgover. To find. "Car Chay dizgovered the Gulfa Sen Lornz in 1534."

·Eeja. To bite fiercely, consume "Cmin quick, Susan, ur the maskiddas ull eeja lyve!"

·Egg spurt. Someone with special skill or knowledge.

·Feudal. Vain or useless. "Leavim lone, Linda. It's feudal tar-gue withim."

·Fishle. Duly authorized. "English and French are the fishle lan-guages of Canada."

·Germ knee. A You're Peen country.

·Hairy. Man's name. "I'm jiss wilda bout Hairy."

# FOUR

## ETHNIC

T HERE are points at which regional, cultural, and ethnic contributions to the language melt in the pot and become indistinguishable. Ethnic strains are treated in this chapter with an eye to the words they have given us, though there is still reference to their own accents. I decided that the place for Black English, as opposed to the traditional Negro dialect in the last chapter, was in the section on fads: though it has a respectable etymological heritage, it appears in many respects to be a political instrument, like feminist English.

The Indians came first . . .

*Algonquian:*

The colonists incorporated Indian words wholesale. A "mugwump" as a fence-sitter and "Podunk" as a one-horse town are pure Algonquian. So are the key words in the following verse:

## THE BIRTHDAY PARTY FOR JOE PAPOOSE

They *powwow* still in the woods of spruce
Of the birthday party for Joe *Papoose.*
The hosts were a *skunk,* a *coon,* and a moose.

The guests were a *woodchuck,* a *caribou,*
A *terrapin* fresh from a Florida slough,
A *chipmunk,* a *possum,* and quite a few

That I've forgotten—all warm, because
Their hosts presented *mackinaws*
And *moccasins.* Two pretty *squaws*

(Whose braves were *sachems*) cooked up a mash
Of hickory nuts and *succotash,*
*Hominy, pemmican,* and such trash,

Including *persimmons, squash,* and *pone.*
They ate all the food that was ever grown,
Then rushed for the *wigwam* all as one.

Since nobody had invented joggin',
The guests rode home on a *toboggan.*


*Chinook:*

Chinook, while certainly a tribe of northwestern Indians, was
also a trading language, with a number of words traceable to
French- and English-speaking trappers. Siwash, for instance, is a
corruption by the Indians of French *sauvage,* and is now considered a derogatory term by some militants. No derogation is intended here.


### SI'S SIWASH LOVE

Lucky Si! his Siwash love
Warms his potlatch on the stove.
Do you say that love is eyewash?
Taste the potlatch of Si's Siwash!
Vittles cooked as she can cook 'em
Skookum ain't—they're super-skookum.
Three now ride on Si's cayuse—
Si and Siwash and papoose!


*Spanish:*

Particularly in the Southwest, many Spanish and Mexican-
Spanish words have been absorbed unchanged into English. Who
would think of calling San Francisco St. Francis, or Los Angeles
The Angels?

We tend to overlook the Spanish origin of such words as alfalfa,
calaboose, chaparral, cinch, cockroach, cork, corral, chaps,
gringo, hoosegow, incommunicado, junta, lariat, marijuana, ma-
chete, mesquite, mosquito, molasses, padre, patio, placer, plaza,
pimento, rodeo, ranch, savvy, sherry, stampede, tornado, vamoose,

and vigilante. Some Spanish words we use without thought for their origin are included in the following verse.

## WHERE SIERRAS RISE FROM MESAS

Where *sierras* rise from *mesas,*
   Out among the western *canyons,*
Senor O.s *adobe* place is;
   It is also his companion's.
Though their food is scant, it's jolly.
No *tortilla?* Try *tamale.*
If *tamale* is too lowly,
There is plenty of *frijole.*
On *fiesta* days they throw
Beans and *chile* in for show.
Hear them joking: *"Compañero,*
I will shoot off your *sombrero!"*
See him playing *Buckaroo:*
See his *lariat lasso*
His *querida,* acting *bronc,*
*Burro, pinto, mustang,* donk.
A *siesta,* stakes are greater:
Which will play the *alligator?*
Can they share those pleasant naps
Without taking off their *chaps?*
Friends report the O.'s a *poco*
(Meaning just a trifle) *loco.*

*French and French Canadian:*

   French words that have settled into English intact except for an occasional shift in pronunciation number in the thousands. I list those that first enter my head: bouillon, bouquet, brassière (bra), camembert, canapé, caprice, chaise, chaperon, chauffeur, chiffonier, claque, cliché, cologne, connoisseur, consommé, coquette, coupé, courtesan, cravat, crêpe, cretin, cretonne, debutante, decolleté, dilettante, ennui, etiquette, fleur-de-lis, hors d'oeuvres, limousine, milieu, mignonette.

   French Canadian, a special dialect represented in the following verse, has given us such words as prairie, bateau, portage, rapids, butte, cache, picayune, chute, coulee, crevasse, depot, and sashay.

## DE NICE LEETLE CANADIENNE

You can pass on de worl' w'erever you lak,
   Tak' de steamboat for go Angleterre,

Tak' car on de State, an' den you come back,
    An' go all de place, I don't care—
Ma frien' dat's a fack, I know you will say,
    W'en you come on dis contree again,
Dere's no girl can touch, w'at we see ev'ry day,
    De nice leetle Canadienne.

Don' matter how poor dat girl she may be,
    Her dress is so neat an' so clean,
Mos' ev'rywan t'ink it was mak' on Paree
    An' she wear it, wall! jus' lak de Queen.
Den come for fin' out she is mak' it herse'f,
    For she ain't got moche monee for spen',
But all de sam' tam, she was never get lef'
    Dat nice leetle Canadienne.

* * *

I marry ma famme w'en I'm jus' twenty year,
    An' now we got fine familee,
Dat skip roun' de place lak leetle small deer,
    No smarter crowd you never see—
An' I t'ink as I watch dem all chasin' about,
    Four boy an' six girl, she mak' ten,
Dat's help mebbe kip it, de stock from run out,
    Of de nice leetle Canadienne.

O she's quick an' she's smart, an' got plain-tee heart,
    If you know correc' way go about,
An' if you don' know, she soon tole you so
    Den tak' de firs' chance an' get out;
But if she love you, I spik it for true,
    She will mak' it more beautiful den,
An' sun on de sky can't shine lak de eye
    Of dat nice leetle Canadienne.

— William Henry Drummond

*German and Pennsylvania Dutch:*
The Pennsylvania Dutch who arrived in colonial times were in
fact Germans. The dialect they developed mixed German with pioneer English. A second river of Germans poured into our country in
the 1840s and 1850s. Our largest single group of immigrants, they
added such words as gesundheit, delicatessen, kindergarten, ouch,
sauerbrauten, stein, wanderlust, hausfrau, zwieback, hamburger,
frankfurter, wienerwurst, schnitzel, and spiel. Academic disciplines
from Germany later accustomed us to such terms as angst and
schadenfreude. Two world wars brought blitzkrieg, panzer, luft-
waffe, stuka, blitz, and flak.

The Dutch, not the Germans, gave rise to a vulgar joke, which I vulgarly pass on. It appears that a Dutch World War II ace was touring the United States to raise money for war bonds. Describing a narrow aerial escape, he recalled with rising excitement, "Dere vas three Fokkers on top of me—three Fokkers on each site— three Fokkers coming up from behint." The chairman interrupted, so as not to confuse the audience: "As you know, a Fokker is a type of German warplane." "Yes!" exclaimed the ace; "but dem Fokkers vas Messerschmidts!"

Though such words as *Himmel, Fräulein, Brot,* and *Stern* in the following verse are German, the dialect comes from the accent and idiom.

## HANS BREITMANN'S PARTY (abridged)

Hans Breitmann gife a barty;
  I vent dere, you'll pe pound.
I valtzet mit Madilda Yane
  Und vent shpinnen round und round.
De pootiest Fraülein in de house,
  She vayed 'pout dwo hoondred pound,
Und efery dime she give a shoomp
  She make de vindows sound.

Hans Breitmann gife a barty;
  I dells you it cost him dear.
Dey rolled in more ash sefen kecks
  Of foost-rate Lager Beer,
Und venefer dey knocks de shpicket in
  De Deutschers gifes a cheer
I dinks dat so vine a barty
  Nefer coom to a het dis year.

Hans Breitmann gife a barty;
  Dere all vas Souse und Brouse;
Ven de sooper comed in, de gompany
  Did make demselfs to house.
Dey ate das Brot und Gensy broost
  De Bratwurst and Braten fine,
Und vash der Abendessen down
  Mit four parrels of Neckarwein.

Hans Breitmann gife a barty—
  Where ish dat barty now?
Where ish de lofely golden cloud
  Dat float on de moundain's prow?

Where ish de himmelstrahlende Stern—
    De shtar of de shpirit's light?
All goned afay mit de Lager Beer—
    Afay in de Ewigkeit!

        —Charles Godfrey Leland

## A DUTCHMAN'S DOG STORY

Der vhas a leedle voman once
    Who keept a leedle shtore,
Und had a leedle puppy dog
    Dot shtoodt pefore der door.
Und evfery dime der peoples coom
    He opened vide him's jaw.
      Schnip! Schnap! shoost so,
        Und bite dem.

Vun day anoder puppy dog
    Cooms runnin' down der shtreet,
Oudt of Herr Schneider's sausage-shop,
    Vhere he had shtoled some meat;
Und after him der Schneider man—
    Der vhind vhas no more fleet.
      Shir-r-r! Whist! shoost so,
        Like vinkin!

Der leedle voman's puppy dog
    Whas lookin' at der fun,
He barkt at der Schneider man,
    Und right pefore him run;
Den fell him down, dot Schneider man,
    Like shooted mit a gun.
      Bang! Crash! shoost so,
        Und voorser.

Der puppy dog dot shtoled der meat,
    Roon'd on und got avhay;
Deer leedle voman's puppy dog
    Der Schneider man did slay,
Und make him indo sausages—
    Dot's vot der peoples say.
      Chip! Chop! shoost so,
        Und sell him.

*Der Moral*

Der moral is, don't interfere
    Vhen droubles is around;

Der man dot's in der fightin' crowd
　　Vhill get hurt I'll be pound.
Mind your own peesness, dot is pest,
　　In life she vhill be found.
　　　　Yaw! Yaw! shoost so,
　　　　　　I pet you.

　　　　　　　　—J. T. Brown

*Irish:*

　　The Irish contribution to our vocabulary is meager, considering the music of their own speech and their masterful use of English. A few familiar words of Irish origin are: smithereen, shillelagh, colleen, speakeasy, shanty, paddy wagon, shebang, limerick, slogan, plaid, blarney, ballyhoo, and shenanigan. Irish immigrants have also been blamed for the convergence in meaning of "I shall" and "I will."

## FINNIGIN TO FLANNIGAN

Superintendent wuz Flannigan;
Boss av the siction wuz Finnigin;
Whiniver the kyars go offen the thrack,
An' muddled up things t' the divil an' back,
Finnigin writ it to Flannigan,
After the wrick wuz all on ag'in;
　　That is, this Finnigin
　　Reported to Flannigan.

When Finnigin furst writ to Flannigan,
He writed tin pages—did Finnigin,
An' he tould jist how the smash occurred;
Full minny a tajus, blunderin' wurrd
Did Finnigin write to Flannigan
Afther the cars had gone on ag'in.
　　That wuz how Finnigin
　　Reported to Flannigan.

Now Flannigan knowed more than Finnigin—
He'd more idjucation, had Flannigan;
An' it wore'm clane an' complately out
To tell what Finnigin writ about
In his writin' to Muster Flannigan.
So he writed back to Finnigin:
　　"Don't do sich a sin ag'in;
　　Make 'em brief, Finnigin!"

When Finnigin got this from Flannigan,
He blushed rosy red, did Finnigin;
An' he said: "I'll gamble a whole month's pa-ay
That it will be minny an' minny a da-ay
Befoore Sup'rintindint—that's Flannigan—
Gits a whack at this very same sin ag'in.
　From Finnigin to Flannigan
　Reports won't be long ag'in.

* * *

Wan da-ay, on the siction av Finnigin,
On the road sup'rintinded by Flannigan,
A rail give way on a bit av a curve,
An' some kyars went off as they made the swerve.
"There's nobody hurted," sez Finnigin,
"But reports must be made to Flannigan."
　An' he winked at McGorrigan,
　As married a Finnigin.

He wuz shantyin' thin, wuz Finnigin,
As minny a railroader's been ag'in,
An' the shmoky ol' lamp was burnin' bright
In Finnigin's shanty all that night—
Bilin' down his repoort, wuz Finnigin!
An' he writed this here: "Muster Flannigan:
　Off ag'in, on ag'in,
　Gone ag'in—FINNIGIN.

—Strickland Gillilan

*Scandinavian:*

　The influx of Scandinavians into the United States began in the 1850s, reaching a peak in the 1880s. Its influence on the language was negligible. Mencken reports, however, that in Minnesota and adjacent states many Swedish and Dano-Norwegian terms are in common use. Swedish gives lutfisk (a fish delicacy), lingon (a berry), and lag (an association of Swedes from the same province). From Dano-Norwegian comes gubbefest (a men's party) and lefsi (a pastry served with coffee). Scandinavian idioms are widely retained, as in "to cook coffee," "forth and back," and "to hold with" (in the place of to agree with).

## SONNET ON STEWED PRUNES

Ay ant lak pie-plant pie so wery vell;
Ven ay skol eat ice-cream, my yaws du ache;
Ay ant much stuck on dis har yohnnie-cake

Or crackers yust so dry sum peanut shell.
And ven ay eat dried apples, ay skol svell
Until ay tenk my belt skol nearly break;
And dis har breakfast food, ay tenk, ban fake:
Yim Dumps ban boosting it, so it skill sell.
But ay tal yu, ef yu vant someteng fine,
Someteng so sveet lak wery sveetest honey,
Vith yuice dat taste about lak nice port vine,
Only it ant cost hardly any money,
Ef yu vant someteng yust lak anyel fude,
Yu try stewed prunes. By yiminy! Dey ban gude.

— William F. Kirk

*Italian:*

Words incorporated into English from Italian include: torso, stanza, vista, incognito, gala, malaria, manifesto, cameo, zucchini, broccoli, influenza, macaroni, spaghetti, pizza, ravioli, espresso, studio, ghetto, buffalo, and ducat. In his *Etymological Dictionary,* Walter William Skeat says that 24 per cent of Italian-born words in English are found in the world of music. Among these are: tempo, aria, alto, piano, pianissimo, crescendo, adagio, intermezzo, staccato, presto, opera, solo, trio, cello, trombone, libretto, segue, coda, obbligato, bravura, virtuoso, and maestro.

Some distortions of English by Italian immigrants are lovingly re-created in the following verse.

## LEETLA GIUSEPPINA

Joe Baratta's Giuseppina
  She's so cute as she can be;
Justa com' here from Messina,
  Weeth da resta family.
Joe had money in da banka—
  He been savin' for a year—
An' he breeng hees wife, Bianca,
  An' da three small children here.
First ees baby, Catarina,
  Nexta Paola (W'at you call
  Een da Inglaise langwadge "Paul"),
  An' da smartest wan of all—
    Giuseppina!

Giuseppina justa seven,
  But so smart as she can be;
Wida-wake at night-time even,
  Dere's so mooch dat's strange to see.

W'at you theenk ees mos' surprise her?
  No; ees no da buildin's tall;
  Eef, my friend, you would be wisa
  You mus' thenk of som'theeng small.
Eet's an ant! W'en first she seena
  Wan o' dem upon da ground,
  How she laughed and danced around:
  "O! 'Formica,' he has found
    Giuseppina!"

"Oh" she cried to heem, "Formica"
  (Dat's Italian name for heem),
"How you getta here so queecka?
  For I know you no can sweem;
An' you was not on da sheepa,
  For I deed not see you dere.
How you evva mak' de treepa?
  Only birds can fly een air.
How you gat here from Messina?
  O' at las' I ondrastand!
You have dugga through de land
  Jus' to find your leetla frand,
    Giuseppina!"

        —T. A. Daly

*Russian and Turkish:*

  Don't try to learn anything from the following verse; it is included, as it was written, just for fun.

## "SOLDIER, REST!"

A Russian sailed over the blue Black Sea
  Just when the war was growing hot,
And he shouted, "I'm Tjalikavakeree—
  Karindabrolikanavandorot—
    Schipkadirova—
    Ivandistova—
      Sanilik—
      Danilik—
    Varagobhot!"

A Turk was standing upon the shore
  Right where the terrible Russian crossed:
And he cried, "Bismillah! I'm Abd el Kor—
  Bazaroukilgonautoskobrosk—
    Getzinpravadi—

Kilgekosladji—
  Grivido—
  Blivodo—
Jenikodosk!"

So they stood like brave men, long and well,
  And they called each other their proper names.
Till the lockjaw seized them, and where they fell
  They buried them both by the Irdosholames—
    Kalatalustchuk—
    Mischaribustchup—
      Bulgari—
      Dulgari—
Sagharimainz.

— Robert J. Burdette

*Yiddish:*

Among Yiddish words that have merged into informal American speech are: kosher, mazuma, shekel, kibitz, bagel, blintz, shnook, schmaltz, schnozzle, lox, shmooz, and shamus. Others, commonly used but still associated with their lingual background, are gonif, meshugge, tochis, gefilte fish, goy, mazel tov, nosh, schiksa, schlemiel, shnook, and shmeer.

## IT RITES PAUL REWERE ON A HUSS HUSSBACK (abridged)

Geeve a leesten mine cheeldren you'll gonna hear
Wott it rilly heppened to Paul Rewere:
On de haiteent from Hapril in savanty-fife—
I tink wot de huss is still alife.
(Occurding mine race-treck retoins lest year.)

He sad to his frand, "Dere's a no-goot boid
Entitled His Mejesty Judge de Toid;
Sotch hideas he gats—wot dey must be de Quinn's
Bot he tinks dees is China und he's de Marinzz!

A welcome we'll geeve heem wot's feet for a Keeng
Far be it from me I should gatting sorrkestic
Bot to motch in de Heaster Parate yat dees Spreeng
He'll nidd foist a hexpoit from soigery plestic.

So climb by de choich in de belfry-hotch
Sleep me de high-sign so soon wot dey motch
Waiting I'll be from de reever acruss
In a seeting position on top from a huss.

Snurtting witt prencing mine nubble bist
From witamines fool like a cake from yist.

De titings will sprad it should stott opp de fighting
To itch fommer brafe we'll distreebute a titing.
Hout like a haroow we'll fly from a bow
Arozzing de contrysite—noo huss, is no??

Steel was de ceety—aslipp was de pipple
   Agog from excitement is Paul witt de stidd—
But Heck! Wot's dees?? Boins a lemp in de stipple.
   He exclaims to de huss, "Forward motch, precidd!"

Knock!! Knock!! by de durrs—it's de bell hout from horder.
"Gat opp averybody inclooting de boarder!!
Wot sutt from beezness I come here rigodding?
You'll find hout tomorrow whan stotts de bombodding!!
To seex meelion Radcoats who'll come witt a weesit
You'll yunn like a dope dere und esk dem WHOOEEZIT??

Prompt in de monnink arrifed a consignment
His Mejesty's suldiers extrimmingly pompous.
A model was itch from a Cockey refinement
Until it commanced witt de Yenkizz de rompos.

Dey shuldered de broomsteecks, binn-shooters dey ludded,
   "You tutt was a juk on de Tea our Emboggo??"
It flew rocks witt stones and tomatiss expludded.
   "Yi yi yi!" sad de Breetish, "Dees must be Chicoggo!"

It never befurr used a harmy sotch tectics
Dey trite on dem hall tings—axcapt chiroprectics.
   How it deed it de Yenkiss rimmains yat a meestery—
   Bot it stends irregoddless de fects in de Heestory!

— Milt Gross

*Chinese:*

   I confess to a certain fogginess about the contributions of Chinese to English. I do recall "No tickee no washee." Someone once told me that yen, as in "to have a yen for," stems from the Chinese; a Chinese in need of Japanese currency might say, "I have a yen for a yen." Kowtow is Chinese, all right; chow and chop-chop are Chinese with a touch of pidgin. I am tempted to dismiss the whole subject in a phrase:

## ON THE EASE OF CHINESE

Chinese difficult? That's hooey.
Simply say: Chow mein; chop suey.

But that would never do, if only because I must perpetuate this
marvel of nonsense:

## RECITED BY A CHINESE INFANT

If-itty-thesi-mow Jays
Haddee ny up-plo-now-shi-buh nays;
   ha! ha!
  He lote in aw dow,
  Witty motti-fy flow;
A-flew-ty ho-lot-itty flays! Hee!

## TRANSLATION

Infinitesimal James
Had nine unpronounceable names; ha! ha!
   He wrote them all down,
   With a mortified frown,
And threw the whole lot in the flames. Hee!

           —Edward Lear

## LINES FROM WANG-TI

Last year my look-see plum-t*l*ee
  all-flower all-same he snow,
This sp*l*ing much plenty snowflake
  all-same he plum-t*l*ee blow
He snowflake fallee, meltee, he *l*ed leaf
  turneee b*l*own,
My makes first-chop sing-song how luck go
  uppy-down.

           —Charles Godfrey Leland

## THE SEQUEL (an excerpt)

I rang the bell and I said to him
Of Tartar origin, standing grim
Behind the portal: "Be pleased to say
To fair Miss Dora that I would pay
  My compliments overdue."

He took my card, and his almond eye
  With cunning lit as he made reply:
  "Miss Dola no shabee you.
Las' week he mally with Captain Hill,
And now he libing in Marysville."

—Daniel Sidney Richardson

*Japanese:*

Some Japanese words that have moved with unchanged meanings into English are included in the verse that follows:

## FOR THE FORMER SHAH OF IRAN: A BRIEF LESSON IN JAPANESE

Hirohito's riding by?
  *Banzai!*
What to do when mullah hits you?
  *Jujitsu!*
Worn from flight, shah? Summon quick, shah,
  *Jinricksha!*
Want to join in dance-girl-play, shah?
  *Geisha!*
Wish to die for Iran, shahzy?
  *Kamikaze!*
Shah, has life uncrowned grown weary?
  *Hara-kiri!*

*Latin:*

Many Latin words have moved unchanged into English. My copy editor has pointed out to me that they cannot correctly be labeled ethnic; but neither are they regional. The italicized words fit well enough here*:

## LOVE'S VACUUM

This *item* mark—a *recipe*
  For you, it, her, or him;
Upon my *affidavit,*
  'Twill double ardor's *vim:*

Since *minimum* response incites
  A *maximum* of moan,
For *stimulus* to kissing,
  Leave kissing quite alone.

* For Latin abbreviations, see page 16.

# ETHNIC POSTSCRIPT

## BETWEEN TWO LOVES

I gotta love for Angela;
　I love Carlotta, too.
I no can marry both o' dem,
　So w'at I gona do?

　　　　—T. A. Daly

The recent American preoccupation with ethnicity is reflected in the increasing frequency of such statements as, "My forebears arrived in the United States five generations ago; I am a Pole"; or, "My great-grandparents swore allegiance to the flag in 1879; I am an Italian."

In a lingual throw-off of this clan mentality, loyalty to ethnic speech patterns may override loyalty to standard English.

Recently, an English teacher named Jerry Cammarato set up a seminar to improve the diction of New York taxi drivers. First, according to Israel Shenker of the New York *Times,* he suggested that the drivers eliminate "toity-toid" and "toid" (*thirty-third* and *third* to you) from their vocabularies. "Uf caws," said a driver in the back row.

Mr. Cammarato's next suggestion was that the flat "a" in apple and other words not be pronounced like a flat "e." "You cannot say epple," he explained earnestly.

Protested a driver, "But, Jerry, I know a lot of people who say 'Give me a epple . . .'"

The reporter draws a veil over Mr. Cammarato's further frustrations, until one Isadore Koenig asks, "In respect to the Oxford English or the King's English, how is this in relation to that?"

At this point the teacher's vocal machine slips out of gear; his lips idle soundlessly. Fortunately, the class is breaking to savor stacks of corned beef. "Not with ya fingehs!" shouts a student. "Don't be a cab driveh!"

It is doubtful whether Mr. Cammarato changed many taxi drivers into Ed Newmans. But in the course of his lecture he made a point that deserves repetition. "We're not asking you," he said, "to pass out of the room when this presentation is over and change your speech pattern. Some of you are going back to the Bronx; some of you are going back to Brooklyn. But if you want to improve your image, take that one extra step."

He meant, I assume, that one determined to rise in the world can learn general English for outside affairs, while retaining at home at least in part English like mother used to make. A tricky balance, to be sure, requiring determination combined with a particularly stable personality. Mike Quill, the Irish-born head of the Transport Workers Union in New York, knew the trick backward and forward; he switched at will between conventional English for formal negotiations and press statements, and the richest Irish brogue when he wished to whip up the enthusiasm of his union members or amuse newsmen.

So not to worry, T. A. Daly. You can marry both Angela and Carlotta, and be happier than you would with either alone. Provided, of course, that you keep them in separate households.

# FIVE

## IDIOMS, COLLOQUIA, AND A FEW TOOTS

W HAT is an idiom? Idioms may be clichés, or slang, or metaphors, or proverbs. They may be single words or whole sentences. They vary from region to region, and from class to class. They may be standard English, dialect, colloquial, or illiterate. They may seem nonsensical or ungrammatical, and be neither.

But whatever their separate attributes, they have one characteristic in common: they defy word-by-word translation into any other tongue. You, dear reader, drank them in at your nursing bottle, or else at your mother's breast. But they are hell on foreigners learning English, because they cannot be deduced; they must be painfully memorized.

And they must be learned exactly. Take idiomatic prepositions. One is "superior to"; one "complies with"—both idiomatically correct. But "superior than" and "comply to"—those are barbarisms.

The root of "idiom" is Greek *idios*, "one's own, peculiar to oneself." (Ironically, the same root is at work in "idiot.") Thus, idioms are a mode of expression peculiar to a given language. Why "feather in one's cap"? "Burn a hole in one's pocket"? "Go by the book"? "Hang fire"? "All wool and a yard wide"? "Apple-pie order"? "Windfall"? "Hammerlock"? "Sunday week"? "Armed to the teeth"? "Eat crow"? "Hand-me-down"? "Lose track"? "A thing or two"? "Two-timer"? "Break the bank"?

You are familiar with the idioms in the following verses. I cite them simply to remind you how much fun they can be.

**GET**  (a rondeau redoublé)

Get gets around. Get also gets the air;
    Gets after; gets it in the neck; gets set.
It gets off easy . . . back at . . . in my hair.
    Prince, marvel at all these: the get of get!

Get gets a wiggle on; gets off the ground; gets wet;
    Gets wise to; gets the gate; gets here; gets there;
Gets words in edgewise . . . wind of . . . even with. You bet,
    Get gets around! Get also gets the air.

Get gets a load of; gets ahead; gets square;
    Gets on the ball (I've hardly started yet).
It gets the worst of; sometime gets unfair;
    Gets after; gets it in the neck; gets set.

Get gets my number; gets me in a fret;
    Gets on my nerves . . . a move on . . . tells me where
I get off; gets a rise out of; gets met;
    It gets off easy . . . back at . . . in my hair.

Get gets along; gets by; gets lost; gets rare;
    Gets better . . . down to cases . . . in a sweat . . .
The jump on . . . to first base . . . me down . . . a threat.
    Prince, marvel at all these: the get of get!

Get gets my back up; gets me out of debt.
    It gets the ax . . . the feel of; gets unbear-
able . . . the picture . . . in a pet . . .
    Me off. It even gets the clothes I wear.
                Get gets around.

**ALL**

It's all to the good to be all ears;
    Thus wisdom comes.
It's all to the bad, though, if one hears
    That one's all thumbs.
All told, and speaking all in all,
    Best be all set—
When all is up with you, you'll fall,
    And be all wet.

* * *

All in a day's work, foe or lover;
All but the shouting's soon all over.

The more colloquial the English, the more idiomatic it is likely to be. The idioms and colloquialisms in the verse below—a ballade with a double refrain—have been around for the last hundred years or more, and are as common as ever today.

## WHEN THE WHOLE BLAMED CABOODLE HAS GONE UP THE SPOUT

When the whole blamed caboodle has gone up the spout;
  When you reckon you've fizzled, and flunked out, and so on;
When your hash has been settled, your string has run out,
  And you figure there's nothing much else left to go on;
When the coin of the realm is the coin that you're low on;
  When you look like a goner, a blooming galoot,
And your dishes are busted, save one to eat crow on—
  *Clink glasses, my brother, and knock back a snoot.*

You have kept your eyes skinned, you have gandered about,
  You have never said die, nor your row ceased to hoe on;
You have hefted your ax, you have tickled your trout,
  And you figure there's nothing much else left to go on;
You have taken life's wallops, and one more to grow on,
  And shut up, and buttoned your lip, and stayed mute.
You're the sort of a fellow I'll wager my dough on—
  *Clink glasses, my buddy, and knock back a snoot.*

So it's root, hog, or die—and you're sore in the snout?
  And it seems a coon's age since you last had a glow on?
(And you're feeling knee-high to a skeeter, no doubt,
  And you figure there's nothing much else left to go on):
I'll risk a simoleon, win, place, or show on
  My hunch you'll still carry on, playing your flute.
Come lickety-split, friend; we've embers to blow on—
  *Clink glasses, good buddy, and knock back a snoot.*

## ENVOY

You know you can't help it, time's river will flow on,
And you figure there's nothing much else left to go on,
But I have a treatment that chaws at the root—
*Clink glashes, ole buddy, an' knock back a shnoot.*

### Fishing
  Colloquial English need not be idiomatic at all, or but slightly, as in the following colloquy between two fishermen*:

* As reported by *Inport,* the in-house publication of the Port of Seattle.

"Hiyamac"
"Lobuddy"
"Binnearlong?"
"Cupplours"
"Ketchenenny?"
"Goddafew"
"Kindarthey?"
"Bassencarp"
"Ennysizetoom?"
"Cuplapowns"
"Hittinhard?"
"Sordalike"
"Wahchoozin?"
"Gobbaworms"
"Fishanonaboddum?"
"Rydonaboddum"
"Whatchadrinkin?"
"Jugajimbeam"
"Igoddago"
"Seeyouaroun"
"Yeahtakideezy"
"Gudluk"

Fishing has contributed such idioms as take the bait, be hooked, a fish story, and the big one that got away. Indeed, most sports and games are represented in one idiom or another: kick the bucket; make the goal; have dibs on; have all one's marbles. Gambling gives us, among others, ace in the hole; busted flush; break the bank; a card up one's sleeve; discard.

*Baseball*

Baseball terms are common, as indicated by John O. Herbold II in this list from *Verbatim:*

· He was born with two strikes against him.
· He couldn't get to first-base with that girl.
· He sure threw me a curve that time.
· I'll take a rain-check on it.
· He went to bat for me.
· I liked him right off the bat.
· He was way out in left field on that one.
· He's a foul ball.
· I think you're way off base on that.
· It was a smash hit.
· Let's take a seventh-inning stretch.
· I hope to touch all the bases on this report.
· Could you pinch-hit for me?
· He doesn't even know who's on first.

· I just call 'em as I see 'em.
· He's only a bush-leaguer.
· Major league all the way.
· We'll hit 'em where they ain't.
· He was safe a mile.
· He has a lot on the ball.
· He really dropped the ball that time.
· We'll rally in the ninth.
· No game's over until the last man's out.

Mr. Herbold adds: "And is there any term in our language more synonymous with failure than 'to strike out'?"

*Words and music*

A book, not simply a chapter, would be insufficient to run through idioms traceable to human activities. I shall mention here only one last field—that of music. The Selmer Company of Elkhart, Indiana, publishes a magazine called *Bandwagon*. The magazine discusses matters that for the most part are of special interest to musicians, which is natural, since Selmer is a company that makes and sells musical instruments. But *Bandwagon* editor Harry Randall contributes one regular feature, "Words and Music," full of surprising tidbits that are also intelligible to the general reader. I thank Mr. Randall for sharing the music-born idioms and origins in the article from which I have abridged below.

The following list, by no means comprehensive, includes phrases so widely used in daily life that it may take a moment to recognize their musical origin:
· Pull out all the stops.
· Ring all the changes.
· Face the music.
· Beat the band.
· High note.
· Song and dance.
· Same old refrain.
· Blow your own horn.
· Strike up the band.
· Ring a bell.
· Ring his bell.
· Ring the bell.
· Clear as a bell.
· Chime in.
· Fit as a fiddle.
· Pay the piper.
· Clarion call.
· In tune with.
· Second fiddle.

- Double in brass.
- Play it by ear.
- Theme song.
- To the tune of.
- Soft pedal.
- Down beat.
- Upbeat.
- Offbeat.
- Pipe down.
- Harp on.

If something is named for another object to which it bears a real or fancied similarity, the new word is not an idiom; but the process is identical. Continues Mr. Randall:

"The distinctive shapes or sounds of musical instruments have given dozens of words and phrases to the language. In the case of the violin it is always the shape, never the sound, and almost always the word is fiddle. You have only to substitute violin for fiddle in any of the following terms to see why. Fiddlehead, for example, is a very descriptive name for a fern frond as it emerges in spring. But violin head?

"Nature provides the fiddler crab, fiddler fish, fiddle neck (a common weed), and fiddlewood, whose botanical name is Citharexylum. (Cithara is Latin for lyre.) Art provides fiddle back chairs, fiddle form sofas, and fiddle pattern silverware. Mariners have acknowledged the instrument with fiddle (that essential rail around the top of a seagoing table), fiddle brace, fiddler's green, and fiddlebow. This last looks nothing like a fiddlestick, and rhymes with prow—appropriately, for that is what it is. The machinist's fiddle bow does look like a fiddlestick, and rhymes with sew. Which brings us to the verb fiddle, a bookbinder's term for stitching, as well as everybody's term for doing nothing useful. We leave you to speculate on the reason for that, along with the reason why violin rather than fiddle is lingo for sub-machine gun.

"You may also want to speculate on the origin of G string, which has thus far eluded the experts. Lutestring, on the other hand, has been traced to lustrine, the type of fabric from which lutestring ribbon is made. It has nothing to do with music.

"Drums are everywhere. On the battlefield they make convenient desks for drumhead courts martial. The guilty are likely to be drummed out of their club as well as their regiment. At sea the top of a capstan is called a drum head, while under the sea, drum fish, ah, drum. Around the base of the Capitol dome is yet another drum—a prosaic term that architects avoid in favor of tambour. In the adjacent office building elder statesmen may favor rolltop, or tambour desks. And whenever there is a chicken in the pot, there will soon be two drumsticks on the table. The steel drum, so called because it looks like a drum, has come full circle with the steel drum, a percussion instrument that neither looks nor sounds like a drum.

Among naturalized musical terms are counterpoint, harmony, overtone, burden, descant, fanfare, orchestrate, tattoo, unison, taps, rataplan, offbeat.† A few, such as glee and brawl, have been so transformed in meaning that their musical origin is scarcely recognizable. Others have been picked up from musicians so recently that their gradual absorption into the general vocabulary can still be observed or traced. Woodshed, play the cracks, five finger exercise, sight read, ad lib, false entrance, cue note, vamp, do a number, cut, get with it, sour note, close enough for jazz, E-flat (meaning small), and swing may or may not ultimately become as standard as play by ear or pull out all the stops. But all are promising candidates, even the slangiest of them having been with us for forty or fifty years. Meanwhile, contemporary jazz and rock musicians are flooding our speech with expressions too new to evaluate and too numerous to catalog.‡

† For musical terms drawn from the Italian (and, zeugmatically speaking, Mr. Randall's article), see page 49.

‡ Copyright 1978, The Selmer Company, Elkhart, Indiana. Reprinted by permission of the author.

# SIX

## SLANG, FADS, AND COUNTER-CULTURE

$M$y long association with the Hermit Hoar has sucked away the marrow of my rigidities about English. The Hermit Hoar finds it ridiculous, for instance, to use a dictionary simply to verify one's verbal prejudices. Having lived a long time, he has seen many locutions pass from sunlight into shadow and back into sunlight again. There is no use, he insists, in fighting battles already lost; far better to accept the least intolerable of what is current, while clinging to personally precious standards—what the oncoming generation would call prejudices or even anachronisms. Such tolerance, he reminds me, is particularly easy in English, which is an informal language, disregarding, for instance, the distinctions between the distant and the intimate (*vous/tu* in French; *Sie/du* in German).

He agrees with David Lodge\* that slang "relieves the inevitable monotony and deadening familiarity of ordinary speech"—is, indeed, the poetry of ordinary speech, casting trite notions into fresh molds. Once it becomes common and familiar, "its days are numbered and it either disappears or is absorbed into the standard language."

"I realize, Willard," he says, "that you were brought up to apply more or less static rules of English. Change comes to you as a

\* *Encounter,* October 1978.

surprise, often unpleasant. The trick is to know when you are licked, and co-opt into the language what you perceive as monsters. Eventually they lose their scales and take on a human look."

I was not thinking about such deep matters as I approached the solemn cell a while back; rather, I was thinking about ice-cold beer. As my hand touched the latch, I was astonished to hear a voice issuing from inside.

Now the Hermit Hoar has neither radio, television, nor visitors. Apart, that is, from me and Uncle Cecil. Uncle Cecil, now ninety-two, does not get about as much as he used to, and speaks even less than he once did, which is to say almost not at all; but occasionally he makes his way by slow stages to the solemn cell. As far as I know, he and the Hermit Hoar never converse at these meetings; they simply rock tranquilly in their respective chairs, the Hermit Hoar proceeding at a leisurely pace through mug after mug of beer while Uncle Cecil nurses his Bourbon and Seven-up. At last Cecil arises, clamps his yellow sou'wester on his head, and slips into his yellow raincoat (it is not always raining in Oysterville, but don't take odds that rain is not falling there at this moment). He says "Good night, Hermit," and squishes back to his home in the village.

The Hermit Hoar is so reclusive, indeed, that I doubt whether most of the villagers know he exists. He never visits the local grocery-post office; once or twice a week, instead, I bring him the necessities of living—soap, bread, and such. He eats mostly from cans, but is pleased by an occasional serving of chicken or beef, dressed in what I think is called sanitary wrapping. He also likes Baldwin apples. Each apple takes him upwards of half an hour to eat. He peels off the skin with a jackknife and then scrapes away the flesh of the fruit with his two top incisors, the only teeth he has left.

He favors also the saucer-sized oysters that grow in the bay fronting Oysterville. I bring him these fresh from the beds, in dripping gunny sacks, but refuse to remain while he prys each shellfish open and slurps down the contents; I cannot stand the sight and smell of the things. Apart from Uncle Cecil, me, and Author Unknown, the Hermit Hoar does not address a word to anyone from year's end to year's end.

Yet here he was, speaking loudly, and in a curious twang; when I rapped and entered, he did not even call over his shoulder, "Come, my lad, and drink some beer."

*CB Lingo:*

A pair of earphones was on his head; a microphone was in his hand. "Step on, Purty Pants," he was saying, in a vile imitation of southwestern accent; "you got John Bull here, looking for that sweet thing."

I sought to interrupt, but he glared at me, so I reeled up the earthenware jug and poured out our beers. My ears were bombarded meanwhile with phrases like "big ears," "bucket mouth," "step on Smokey's toes," "go juice," "cackle crate," and "dead pedal." When I handed him his mug, he said into the microphone, "Back out, Purty Pants; a good buddy just come in with a brew. Catch you on the flip-flop." He then removed his earphones, snapped off the transmission device beside his rocking chair, blew the barm from his beer, took his usual deep swig, and regarded me with a benign countenance.

"Hermit Hoar," said I, "have you gone out of your mind?"

"Bring it back," said the Hermit Hoar.

"Bring back what?"

"Repeat transmission. Come again."

"I said, have you gone out of your mind?"

"Pass another brown bottle, good buddy. You're talking to a big rigger."

"To a what?"

"A dude that operates a growed-up truck. An eighteen-wheeler. At least that's what my CB buddies think I am."

"What's an eighteen-wheeler?"

"A forty-footer. A truck with eighteen wheels."

"And what do you mean by your CB buddies?"

"Users of Citizens Band radio to you—mostly drivers of trucks, campers, and ordinary cars. More than eleven million of us are licensed and we walk the dog day and night."

"Walk the dog?"

"Operate the CB set. More cold coffee?"

"Coffee?" I echoed, peering into my empty mug. "You never drank coffee in your life."

"*You* call it beer," said the Hermit Hoar.

"What do eleven million of you have to discuss?"

"Mostly we give bear reports."

"Is there a connection between truck drivers and bears?"

"Bears are police, my lad. A speeding motorist is bear bait—bear food—bear meat. A bear in the bushes is a speed trap. Bears wall-to-wall are police all over the place."

I protested, "But the only bears within twenty miles of the solemn cell go on four legs. What do *you* have to warn truck drivers about?"

"I can pretend, can't I? When I say, 'Bears be in those bushes,' everyone slows down." A light began blinking on the set. He picked up his microphone, and said, "You got John Bull here, good buddy. What's your handle? Sure you're not abusing it, Undercover Lover? Choking the chicken, maybe? No harm intended, good buddy. You don't sound like no Three-legged Beaver to me. What's your twenty? Brush your teeth and comb your hair, lover; they's honey on the road. Better hammer off—double nickel for a while. Well, I gotta cut loose. Have a 36-24-36, old buddy."

"And what was that all about?"

"We CB communicators are rough of tongue, my lad. All in good fun, though. 'Abusing it,' 'choking the chicken'—masturbation, of course. All alone in that big cab, you can't blame a man, can you?

"In CB lingo," he went on, " 'Three-legged Beaver' is a homosexual. 'What's your twenty?' is what's your location. 'Brush your teeth and comb your hair' means there's police radar ahead. 'Hammer off' is slow down; 'double nickel' means fifty-five miles an hour; 'cut loose' is sign off; '36-24-36' is good night. Which reminds me that CB has proved a gold mine for the pavement princesses."

"The—?"

"Hag bags. Bra busters. Dresses for sale. Free rides. Little bits. Muffs. San Quentin jailbait. Trick babes."

"Meaning whores?"

"Clever of you to catch on. They use CB to set up appointments at truck stops. Too bad I don't have a rig."

When he had wearied of his act, the Hermit Hoar told me a few facts about CB. The first purpose of the amateur network was to aid truckers in trouble, to act as a warning against police traps, and to report road conditions. Gradually, CB has grown into a nationwide personal communications link, lacking the responsibility of actual personal meeting. Educated men and women assume truckers' jargon to talk on CB, choosing handles like Irish Bootlegger, Ohio Knucklehead, and Country Bumpkin.

CB vocabulary has at least twenty-one words for a wife, as distinguished from a companion of the moment. They range from better half to cover, first sergeant, frilly blouse, mini-skirt, old lady, other half, old woman (OW), panty-stretcher, beaver, and super skirt. On another level, the expressions for coffee include cup of mud, black water, and thirty-weight.

"A new dialect, my lad," said the Hermit Hoar, rubbing his hands.

"You have been a prototypical Englishman for hundreds of years. Do you propose to talk now with truckers' twang and jargon?"

"You have always underestimated me, lad. You may yet see me waving to you from the cab of a growed-up truck."

"Are you insinuating that even CB may someday add its pittance to standard English?"

"I make no prophecies. The terms may go the way of jazznik, protestnick, of ecohead, a togetherperson, and growthsmanship. Or they may endure, like in thing, fun thing, and doing one's own thing. As I said before, the proletariat will propose, and the elite dispose; the only difficulty is that it is so hard to tell these days which is which."

"Then you will not accept the ban of a Fowler or a Follett?"†

"If they bend to the wind, lad; if they bend to the wind. Have another beer."

From then on, his diction returned to that of the Hermit Hoar I had always known. Still, I was relieved on my next visit to find that the CB antenna had been removed from the roof of the solemn cell.

*Women's Lib:*

As far as I know, the interest of the Hermit Hoar in women as women is academic. He is sex-blind. I, on the other hand, though I fight constantly to liberate myself from antisocial sexism, would find intolerable a world where women for men, and men for women, were not sex objects. That the pull of one sex toward the other lessens either escapes my logic. As far as I am concerned, women are human beings with the added fillip of sex, and that is all there is to it.

Anyhow, the Hermit Hoar ardently backs the women's movement; he even corresponds at long intervals with Betty Friedan.

"Ours has been a patriarchal society since man knoweth not to the contrary," he remarked one day. "And the key word in that sentence is 'man.' It is both a collective for all human beings and a designation for one half of them—the males. Woman, on the other hand, stands for a half but not the whole. As the grammatical witticism observes, 'man embraces woman.'"

"You have been reading feminist literature again," I said.

"I certainly have. And I agree with it. Words and expressions implying male superiority pervade the language. Women are likely to be described simply in physical terms, or characterized in a pejorative way implying, say, weakness, duplicity, or temptation."

"You mean that dictionaries define man as the plum and woman as the prune?"

"Not in the vulgar epithets you use; but that is the general idea. Words for things we like tend to take on a male aura; those we dislike turn female."

"I never call my sloop anything but she, yet I am very fond of boats," I said.

"An exception only proves the rule. No, women have a very good case as long as they do not try to turn themselves into men,

† H. W. Fowler and Wilson Follett are well-known authorities on English usage.

which few do. But they put it badly. Will Shakespeare summarized part of their problem more eloquently than any of them have managed to do for themselves. Do you remember when Brutus, brooding over his participation in the plot to assassinate Caesar, refuses to tell his wife Portia what is bothering him? Says Portia:

"Within the bond of marriage, tell me, Brutus,
  Is it excepted I should know no secrets
  That appertain to you? Am I yourself,
  But, as it were, in sort or limitation,
  To keep with you at meals, comfort your bed,
  And talk to you sometimes? Dwell I but in the
      suburbs
  Of your good pleasure? If it be no more,
  Portia is Brutus's harlot, not his wife."

"All perfectly true," I said. "But it seems to me that women become laughable and hurt their own cause when they actually set out to reshape overnight a language whose roots go back ten thousand years. The chickens won't fly."

I happened to be agitated at that moment, because I had just been studying certain instructions circulated by McGraw-Hill, the publishing house, among nonfiction writers. The idea was to eliminate such presumably sexist and patronizing terms as the fair sex, a goddess on a pedestal, woman driver, scatterbrained female, and the like, while praising in women such traditionally male virtues as boldness, initiative, and assertiveness.

I had tried to write a love poem, incorporating these guidelines, and had failed miserably:

### A SWEET YOUNG THING'S MY TRUE LOVE

A sweet young thing's my true love;
  She's of the fairer sex—
Appropriately slender,
  Agreeably convex.
My true love's kisses carry
  A jolt like usquebaugh;
How I would love to praise her
  For Hill and for McGraw!

Her gentleness, compassion,
  And tenderness I sing;
She does drive like a woman,
  But you can't have everything.

A fragile flower my love is,
  A gem without a flaw—
A subject in a thousand
  For Hill and for McGraw:

A goddess on an altar,
  A blushing rose unstained,
And maybe just a teeny,
  Wee bit scatterbrained.
She'll soon my better half be . . .
  My little woman . . . squaw.
Why, they should stop the presses
  At Hill and at McGraw!

If she were an accountant,
  Or ran a power saw,
They'd slaver for her story
  At Hill and at McGraw.
If she were tough, assertive,
  With thrusting underjaw,
She'd sell a million copies
  For Hill and for McGraw.

But she likes pretty dresses.
  Does anybody know
How sexist terms are doing
  At Harper and at Row?

## MS

A number of the words developed for purposes of women's liber-
ation are too artificial to be taken seriously. At least one knows
the origin of some, such as "chairperson"; but the only word
with a long life expectancy coined by the movement is Ms, which,
though an abbreviation of nothing, does fill a hole in the language.
Ms is the hero, or the heroine, of the following celebration of abbreviations. In the verse below, St has to be pronounced "st," Ave,
"av"; Sq, "sq"; and Mr. "murr." Motherless Ms, however, is to be
pronounced "mizz." How that pronunciation was arrived at, Ms
only knows.

## PORE LITTLE MS

Abbreviations need a ma,
  Pore little fellers!
When a baby lamb goes "Baa,"
  When a baby heifer bellers,
Ma is there, and—quick as tunket—

Where's her milk? The baby's drunk it.
St's ma is Street, or maybe Saint.
Both will do.
And Ave's (as you may know or mayn't)
Is Avenue.
I could go on like that there:
Sq has a mama, namely Square,
While Mr's ma's Mister.
Golly gee!
Gee whiz!
Pore little Ms!
I wonder who your mama is!


*Cockney rhyming slang:*

The Hermit Hoar beats me all hollow at Cockney rhyming slang. On the other hand, my vocabulary of cowboy slang is more complete than his. Neither the one nor the other is likely to become a staple of normal drawing room conversation, but at least they provide illuminating examples of how circumstances change the spoken language.

Cockney rhyming slang consists of a series of codes, originally used as a criminal argot to outwit the police. Rhyming slang, says Sydney T. Kendall in *Up the Frog,* "usually takes the form of two or three words, the last of which rhymes with the original word. Thus 'stairs' becomes 'apples and pears'; 'collar,' ''oller boys 'oller.' In many instances the slang is shortened to the first word only; 'taters in the mould' (cold) becomes simply 'taters.' This shortened version is used considerably in conversation and is, to say the least, very misleading to a stranger."

"Try this one," says the Hermit Hoar: " 'Two weeks be'ind wiv the *duke* and I ain't got no *bees.'* "

"The only part that means anything to me is 'two weeks be'ind,' " I say. "Rent, maybe?"

"You're on the scent. The longer version is: 'Two weeks be'ind wiv the *Duke o' Kent* and I ain't got no *bees 'n' 'oney.'* "

"Now it comes clear. 'Kent'—rent. ''Oney'—money. 'Two weeks behind with the rent and I ain't got no money.' "

"Excellent. Now try, 'Bung it in the *Johnny* 'longside the *dickory.'* "

"I think I have part of it. 'Dickory.' Dickory dock. Clock. But what's the 'Johnny'?"

"Johnny 'Orner—little Jack Horner."

"Horner—mourner. No, corner. 'Put it in the corner alongside the clock.' "

"You must have been born within sound of the Bow bells," says the Hermit Hoar admiringly.

Ordinarily I do less well. The Hermit Hoar recited the following story in both the shorter and longer versions, but the only words I could identify were the same old rent, corner, and clock.

> "My *one an' t'other* sez, 'I've got a *birch* rahn the *Johnny,'* 'e sez. 'Come in an' 'ave a drop o' *pimple.'*
>
> "So I goes along wiv 'im an' 'e gets aht a *Jennie* an' in we goes into this 'ere *birch* 'e's got.
>
> "There was everythink in it—a *Cain* wiv three *Scotches* on it, a *la-di* over on one side wiv all the *tumbles* you could think of; three *Owens* wiv chalks an' all, an' a 'lectric *dickory* on the mantelpiece over the *Jeremiah.* 'E'd got a *Nervo* in the *burnt,* an' to top the lot a flippin' *Joanna!* An' 'e's only the *Artful!* I bet that little lot costs 'im a packet—then 'e's got the *Duke* on top o' that lot! Cor! 'E must be rollin' in it!"

The Hermit Hoar found it reasonable that I should draw a blank on this shorter version, which left even some of the key rhyming words unspoken; but he did not see why I could not follow the story when all the rhymes were included. It goes like this:

> "My *one an' t'other* sez, 'I've got a *birch broom* rahn the *Johnny 'Orner,'* 'e sez. 'Come in an' 'ave a drop o' *pimple and blotch.'*
>
> "So I goes along wiv 'im an' 'e gets aht a *Jennie Lee* an' in we goes into this 'ere *birch broom* 'e's got.
>
> "There was everythink in it—a *Cain an' Abel* wiv three *Scotch pegs* on it, a *la-di-dah* over on one side wiv all the *tumble-dahn the sink* you could think of; three *Owen Nares* wiv *chalk farms* an' all, an' a 'lectric *dickory dock* on the mantelpiece over the *Jeremiah.* 'E'd got a *Nervo & Knox* in the *burnt cinder,* an' to top the lot a flippin' *Joanna!* An' 'e's only the *Artful Dodger!* I bet that little lot costs 'im a packet—then 'e's got the *Duke o' Kent* on top o' that lot! Cor! 'E must be rollin' in it!"

When the Hermit Hoar finally deigned to explain, the story did not amount to much. Here are the translations:
- *One an t'other* = brother.
- *Birch,* short for "birch broom" = room.
- *Pimple,* short for "pimple and blotch" = scotch.
- *Jennie,* short for "Jennie Lee" = key.
- *Cain an' Abel* = table.
- *Scotch,* short for "Scotch pegs" = legs.
- *La-di,* short for "la-di-dah" = bar.
- *Tumbles,* short for "tumbles down the sink" = drink.

- *Owens,* short for "Owen Nares" = chairs.
- *Chalks,* short for "chalk farms" = arms.
- *Jeremiah* = fire.
- *Nervo,* short for "Nervo & Knox" = box (television set).
- *Burnt,* short for "burnt cinder" = winder.
- *Joanna* = piano.
- *Artful,* short for "artful dodger" = lodger.

*Cowboy slang:*

Cowboy slang has none of the code features of Cockney; what the two dialects share is indelicacy. I am not going to tell you the indecent meanings in Cockney of allfor, almond, alphonse, bolt, bottle, braces, brighton, bristols, and dozens more. At least the Cockneys have the decency to disguise their indecencies. Not so the cowboy of my grandparents' day; and though his descendants may be more at home in the saddle of a jeep than a bronc, their language has not changed. A fast gal, to a cowboy, is one of them widows as always wants her weeds plowed under; she must think her butt is a gold mine since everybody's a-diggin' at it; she has no trouble gettin' a rake to gather her hay crop. Good friends are thicker than calf splatter; deceitful beans is them as talk behind your back; a homely person looks sour enough to pucker a hog's butt, or like the east end of a westbound mule; death is as shore as a belch after a big meal; an unwashed man is shore considerably whiffy on the lee side; a parsimonious man is tighter'n a Scotch maiden on a cold winter night; the most useless objects in existence are tits on a boar pig, and the most useless act is putting a milk bucket under a bull.

There are of course more polite expressions, too, like nothin' to do but stand 'round an' scratch his seat, but they are reserved for Sundays at church.

*Laid back:*

Supreme Court Justice Potter Stewart says he may not be able to define pornography, but he knows it when he sees it. I can't explain laid-back English, but I know when I am hearing or reading it. An outstanding expert on this dialect, which some consider deliberate cultural sabotage, is a young woman named Cyra McFadden, who for a number of years studied laid-back English—language of the "affluent, progressive, trend-haunted, and fad-obsessed Californians"—in its native haunts across the Golden Gate bridge from San Francisco. The following example is from her hilarious and terrifying book *The Serial:*

> "Kate told her friends how happy she was that she and Harvey had decided to split for awhile, because it would give

them a chance to get clear, and because her philosophy, like Sartre's, was that everybody was ultimately responsible for his own number.

"She was even laid back, at least publicly, about Harvey's liaison with Marlene, the eighteen-year-old Safeway checker he was living with in that plastic condo in Greenbrae. If Harvey thought getting it on with some bubble-gum rocker was realizing his full human potential, well, that was his prerogative—though she *was* disappointed that he'd go that route because it was all so predictable. Every husband Kate knew took up with some little postadolescent with acne as soon as he split from his wife . . ."

R. D. Rosen named this strange tongue Psychobabble, and the term appears likely to stick. Here is a further example, as translated by Christopher Reed:

*The Psychobabble:* Hear me. I mean, no way I'm about to lay a bad trip on you. I'm not coming down, like heavy duty, on value judgments. You know the parameters and where it's at. If you've got your head together, you'll know where I'm coming from. You into my space? Wow! I'm really into, you know, I mean how you went with your initial crisis reaction. Aww-right!

*The Translation:* I don't want to disturb you with grave intellectual opinions. But I'm sure, with your understanding, you will grasp my point of view. I'm delighted you can accept this without any upset. Splendid!

Now you or I might regard such fools' jargon as the ultimate degradation of spoken English. But not the Hermit Hoar. At the risk of repeating myself, he has lived longer than we have. It stands to reason, he says, that Psychobabble is spreading because it meets a linguistic need—one in which, perhaps, we see ourselves as caught up in a process of incessant readjustment to new conditions. When the need passes, so will the jargon. Meanwhile, absurd and pretentious as it may be, it reflects one facet of middle-class lives.

*Black English and the counter-culture:*

Quite apart from its regional and ethnic roots, Black English is a political and cultural manifestation. Clarence Major in the *Dictionary of Afro-American Slang* calls it "a whole sense of violent unhappiness in operation." He even argues that American slang in general tends to be black in origin—a code language created by a people with a need for secrecy. In this interpretation, black slang includes prison slang, the language of the black musician, and indeed almost any oral expression of counter-culture. Bad means good; kill, to fascinate; a love letter, a bullet; murder, approval of something excellent.

Jim Haskins and Hugh F. Butts in *The Psychology of Black Language* describe a form of verbal bantering among black children called "signifying," used, they say, for "putting down" another person, making another person feel better, or simply expressing one's own feelings. The following examples are from the black militant H. "Rap" Brown:

- Man, I can't win for losing.
- If it wasn't for bad luck, I wouldn't have no luck at all.
- Can't kill nothing and won't nothing die.
- If I had your hands I'd give 'way both my arms.
- I'm the man but you the main man.
- I read the books you write.

Ralph Ellison, whose judgment on English, black, white, or green, I will accept before that of most men, says that slang deriving from prison and from music was the product of prisoners and musicians, regardless of their race. Much of what is referred to as Black English is simply the counter-culture speaking. Black, criminal, and jazz argot was reinforced in the 1960s, reflecting the disturbances and disaffections of the period. Like long hair and jeans, they were used by the alienated to put the complacent in their place. As always, in the irritating way the complacent have, they wound up by taking over the expressions that were supposed to destroy them. Though the 1970s have produced no such outburst of neologisms, these of the previous decade persist. The following terms may well be part of your next conversation:

Bad vibes. From bad vibrations—an intuition that a group or situation is unsympathetic or threatening.
Into. Occupied with, pursuing the study of: "She's into ESP."
Freak out. Lose control, as under the influence of a drug.
Groove. Ecstasy. "I groove on you." Also move or get together, as in dancing beautifully.
Bust (verb). Arrest, esp. for drugs, campus unrest.
Head (noun). A habitual user of hallucinogens. 2. By extension, any kind of enthusiast, e.g., wordhead = word enthusiast.

The following verse, growing as it went along, appeared in many newspaper columns in the 1960s.

## GROOVY, MAN, GROOVY

Remember when hippy meant big in the hips,
And a trip involved travel in cars, planes, and ships?
When pot was a vessel for cooking things in

And hooked was what grandmother's rug might have been?
When fix was a verb that meant mend or repair,
And be-in meant merely existing somewhere?
When neat meant well organized, tidy, and clean,
And grass was a ground cover, normally green?
When lights and not people were switched on and off,
And the Pill might have been what you took for a cough?
When camp meant to quarter outdoors in a tent,
And pop was what the weasel went?
When groovy meant furrowed with channels and hollows
And birds were wing'd creatures, like robins and swallows?
When fuzz was a substance, real fluffy, like lint,
And bread came from bakeries—not from the mint?
When square meant a 90-degree angled form,
And cool was a temperature not quite warm?
When roll meant a bun, and rock was a stone,
And hang-up was something you did with a phone?
When chicken meant poultry and bag meant a sack,
With junk trashy cast-offs and old bric-a-brac?
When jam was preserves that you spread on your bread,
And crazy meant balmy, not right in the head?
When cat was a feline, a kitten grown up,
And tea was a liquid you drank from a cup?
When swinger was someone who swung in a swing,
And pad was a soft sort of cushiony thing?
When way out meant distant and far, far away,
And a man couldn't sue you for calling him gay?
When tough described meat too unyielding to chew,
And making a scene was a rude thing to do?
Words once so sensible, sober, and serious
Are making the freak scene, like psychodelirious.
It's groovy, man, groovy, but English it's not.
Methinks that our language is going to pot.

— Anonymous


Edmund Wilson, the literary critic, approached the evolution of
the language from a different direction:

## THE PURIST'S COMPLAINT‡

*Jejune, transpire, ilk, demean*
Don't mean what you think they mean—
    Nor *viable*,
    Nor *friable*,
Do look them up, old bean.

‡ From Wilson's *Christmas Stocking*.

And do take pity, if it's not too late,
On *titivate* confused with *titillate*.

—And yet, it's undeniable
These meanings that are gross mistakes
Are creeping in the lexicons
Beside the old authentic ones,
Which may fade out beside the fakes.
    And this, I am afraid,
Is how the languages are made.

# SEVEN

## ERROR, CONFUSION, AND JARGON

YOU would not have come this far with me if you were not reasonably comfortable with spoken English. Doubtless you catch yourself in an occasional slip, the kind all flesh is heir to, and I hope that as you pause over the verses that litter this book you will learn slips to avoid. But though you should speak meticulously, you should do so without self-consciousness, or you will simply sound silly. And if your speech becomes precious, you will be like a horse with a broken leg; out of kindness, you should be shot.

If you speak well, you will pray well. This advantage increases your chances of heaven, and is alone worth the price you paid for my book.

Scientific studies indicate that good speech is helpful even here on earth. It is said to help one win at bingo, horse races, and lotteries. But be cautious about taking my word on this; the final evidence is not in. If you are an unattached woman, good English will help you win the man of your choice, provided you also stop chewing gum. If you are an unattached man, it will help you win the woman you love, provided you stop jogging.

Errors sprout like dandelions in the verses that make up much of *Say It My Way*. No one of them is calamitous. Too many errors, though, signify a poorly tended lawn.

*Malapropisms:*

Among these errors is the malapropism. If instead of saying, "Errors sprout like dandelions," I had said, "Errors spout like dandelions," I would have been malapropping. Malapropisms, being largely an affliction of the semi-literate, are not likely to represent a problem for you. Still, once they take root, they are as hard as dandelions to eradicate. Keep your trowel handy.

Named after Mrs. Malaprop, in Sheridan's comedy *The Rivals,* malapropism describes a class of mistake that consists of saying an unrelated word very similar in its sound to the one the speaker presumably is groping for. Mrs. Malaprop was said to "deck her dull chat with hard words which she don't understand." An allusion to the past became for her a "delusion to the past." "If I reprehend anything in this world," she said, "it is the use of my oracular tongue, and a nice derangement of epitaphs." I leave it to you to decide the words she did not quite have in mind.

"Fortuitous" for fortunate, a "shrewd awakening" for a rude awakening, "this is the crutch [rather than the crux] of the problem"—these are malapropisms. It is not difficult to confuse "mendicity," which means begging, with "mendacity," which means lying; or "turbid," which means roiled, with "turgid," which means swollen or distended.

The verse below contains twelve malapropisms, and two other errors belonging to the same general species. All are corrected in the version immediately following. If the first verse makes as much sense to you as the second, either you or I should go back to school.

## WITH GNARLING FINGERS (a sonnet: version 1)

Dear Youth:
    With gnarling fingers I indict
  This plea: pray, scorn me not that I am poor
  With age. Adjure aspersions. I abjure
You: gouge on youth, as is your youthful right,
Ere age shall gorge your cheeks, and dim your sight;
  But do not me indite who scuff, unsure—
  Whose gaps of truth pretend that moment dure
When tooth eternal meets paternal light.

Do not abrade me, youth, that I am old,
For age must each upbraid, you being one.
Portend not: e'en now o'er you creeps the cold—
For which blame time, not me; blame time alone.

Men duly die: then dies discomfit duly.
Wherefore discomfort time, not me.

Yours truly—

## WITH GNARLING FINGERS (a sonnet: version 2)

Dear Youth:
    With gnarling fingers I indite
  This plea: pray, scorn me not that I am poor
  With age. Abjure aspersions. I adjure
You: gorge on youth, as is your youthful right,
Ere age shall gouge your cheeks, and dim your sight;
  But do not me indict, who scuff, unsure—
  Whose gaps of tooth portend that moment dure
When truth eternal meets eternal light.

Do not upbraid me, youth, that I am old,
For age must each abrade, you being one.
Pretend not: e'en now o'er you creeps the cold—
For which blame time, not me; blame time alone.

Men duly die: then dies discomfort duly.
Wherefore discomfit time, not me.

Yours truly—

    I have cheated on some of the barbarisms above; tooth-truth, for instance, is not a true malapropism, which ordinarily implies not affectation, but a mere slip of the tongue. Other malapropisms in the poem are adjure-abjure, abrade-upbraid, pretend-portend, and discomfit-discomfort. Discomfit-discomfort might be better listed, however, as a homonym as is certainly the case with indict-indite.

    Decide on the word replaced by each of the malapropisms or homonyms below. Write the word of your choice in the blanks in the right-hand margin. The correct answers follow.

### R.I.P.

1. The *epigram* upon my stone will say,       _____
2. "No more he *gambles* lamb-like in the sun,     _____
3. For he has *gamboled* his poor life away      _____
      At *Vingt-et-un*.
4. Cleaned out at last, he drank a *vile* of        _____
        strychnine
        So sick'nin'

5. He had to *exercise* it down the john.
   This cleaned him out again, and he was gone.
      Death would have been easier
6.    From milk of *amnesia*." _____

Words malapropped:
1. *Epitaph.* An epitaph is an inscription on a tomb. An epigram is a pithy saying.
2. *Gambol.* To skip about; frolic. To gamble is to wager on an uncertain outcome.
3. *Gamble.* See above.
4. *Vial.* A small glass vessel or phial. Vile means depraved or impure.
5. *Exorcise.* To drive away, as evil spirits. To exercise is to practice or use exertion.
6. *Magnesia.* A purgative. Amnesia is loss of memory.

If you are still in the mood, try your hand at these easy malapropisms:

1. It was the best *piazza* I ever tasted. _____
2. Most of us brush our teeth in the *laboratory*. _____
3. Gorillas have never heard of *gorilla* warfare. _____
4. Go wash; your face is *dinghy!* _____
5. I had raspberry *mouse* for dinner, and gained a pound. _____
6. Raise your *goblins,* and toast the queen! _____
7. She's forgotten her lipstick. What a *calliope!* _____
8. This *carousel* will protect you from the sun. _____

Words malapropped:
1. *Pizza.* A doughy crust with cheese, tomato sauce, and spiced meats. A piazza is a square open place surrounded by buildings, or, loosely, a verandah.
2. *Lavatory.* A place for washing. A laboratory is commonly a place where scientific experiments are performed.
3. *Guerrilla.* Literally, a little war—one carried on by independent bands of armed men. A gorilla is the nearest to man of the great apes.
4. *Dingy.* Dirty, soiled. A dinghy is a type of rowboat.
5. *Mousse.* A rich, generally gelatinized custard of various flavors. A mouse is a small rodent.
6. *Goblets.* Large drinking vessels without a handle. A goblin is a usually malicious fairy.
7. *Catastrophe.* A great misfortune. A calliope is an arrangement of whistles toned to make musical notes.

8. *Parasol*. A shade designed to protect from the sun, as an umbrella from the rain. A carousel is a musical merry-go-round.

## INIQUITY, UNIQUITY

Iniquity . . . uniquity . . .
 I met them in my prime.
Two words whose sense did not agree;
 They did not even rhyme.
Yet each outdid the other in
 Its shrill vituperation
When summing up my state of sin—
 My ultimate damnation.

Uniquity is not extreme naughtiness, but uniqueness; iniquity is not uniqueness, but extreme naughtiness, wickedness. The above verse is a brag; I am implying that in my youth I was unique in iniquity. The fact is that I was the goodest goody-goody on the block.

## ALLUSION, ILLUSION, DELUSION

In this brief poem, there will be
Two words alluded to . . . no, three;
Allusion (1), means "reference";
Illusion (2), "brief want of sense";
Delusion (3), "aberrance fixed."

Let not such niceties be mixed;
Illusion is a slight mistake,
Green apple causing bellyache.
Delusion's worse: If in your brain
You turn into a railway train,
And hit a cow upon the track,
You'll have to pay the farmer back.

I've made to (1), (2), (3), allusion
To end grammatical confusion.

    WRONG: The actor created the delusion that he was Hamlet.
    He is a liar; I have no allusions about him.
    His illusion was that he knew how to sing.

RIGHT: He suffered from the delusion that he
was a green apple.
He made a disparaging allusion to his
professor.
What man believes he knows is illusion.

## FRIABLE, FRANGIBLE (a sonnet)

(After Polonius' farewell to Laertes)

Aboard, Laertes, and my blessing carry;
And let these precepts in thy mem'ry sit
When judging thy familiars. Be thou chary
Of tongues that scuff in slipshod counterfeit,
Their words being unproportion'd to their thought:
Ill-said is no less ill because intangible.
Give every man thy ear. But count him naught
Who friable equates with frangible,
Since friable is foreordained to crumble,
While frangible is brittle, and must shatter.
From trope to trope do men, like drunkards,
    stumble,
And make of synonyms identic matter.

Reserve thy love for the punctilious few.
I wouldn't count on more than one or two.

Most of us do not use friable or frangible often. Still, there is
no harm in bearing the distinction in mind:

Friable (adjective). Easily or readily crumbled.
Frangible (adjective). Fragile; brittle.

## NAUSEOUS, NAUSEATED

"I'm nauseous," to be precise,
  Means "I am loathsome." My advice,
When you must whoops, is simply stated:
Cry, "Gangway! I am nauseated!"

Nauseous (adjective). Disgusting; tending to
excite nausea.
Nauseated (predicate adjective). Feeling nausea; inclined to vomit.

*Homonyms:*
Homonyms, words with the same sounds but different spellings

and meanings, are easily distinguishable in speech by context and intonation. There are thousands of them. Most are twins: ate, eight; blew, blue; red, read; and so on. Triplets flourish: by, buy, bye; crews, cruise, cruse; heal, heel, he'll; idle, idol, idyl; and there are quadruplets: cere, sear, seer, sere. Quintuplets and even sextuplets are doubtless waiting in the wings. Mine (a place where ore is obtained), and mine (belonging to me) are not homonyms, but identicals; they are spelled the same.

The same word may have different meanings, depending on context, inflection, emphasis, facial expression, and the like. "Heave" changes considerably here:

## THE HEAVING OF HER MAIDEN BREAST

The heaving of her maiden breast
  Had to be seen to be believed.
The boat lurched down another crest . . .
  And up she heaved.

Another pair:

## EXCEPT, ACCEPT, AND AX

Except (a verb that means "leave out")
May turn into a preposition.
Accept (a verb that means "receive")
Is limited to one condition.
"Accept for me, all men are dense,"
Though true, defies intelligence.

I begged your hand, when hotly waxed
My love; yet I could scarce believe
You when you answered: "Do you ax
Henceforth to merge our income tax?
Come, kiss me, dear, for I except."
Did you mean yes? or no? I wept,
While love went flying up the spout.
Yet you had mentioned ax. I crept
Into the chamber where you slept.
And axed you, as you'd axed.

WRONG: "I except your hand in marriage."
RIGHT: "I accept your hand in marriage."

To say "ax" for "ask" is a barbarism, and I hope I won't have to speak to you about it twice.

## IDOL, IDLE

This homonymic verse slipped in by accident.

My idol!—your idle
    Tears drown my poor heart;
Why bridle, when bridal
    Delights I'd impart?
Think not from your side'll
    I sidle, my pet;
This idyll that died'll
    Revive for us yet.
All loving is tidal,
    Each tide'll go slack—
Yet if we but bide, 'll
    Come fresheting back.

## PITCHER, PICTURE

My pitcher and my picture I can hardly
    tell apart;
My pitcher has but little spout, my
    picture little art.

PREFERRED: For pitcher: PICH-ər
                  For picture: PIK-chər

See p. 169 for pronunciation of the schwa (ə).

## CONSUMMATE

When our desire is so in spate
That we one flesh become, it
Is the *act* we CON-sum-māte;
The *pleasure* is con-SUM-it.

PREFERRED: (adjective): cən-SUM-ĭt
                  (verb): cŏn-sə-MĀT

Check your preferred definitions below:

CONSUMMATE (adjective)  1. clever
                                    2. feverish
                                    3. complete; perfect
                                    4. capable of being
                                        consumed

CONSUMMATE (verb)
1. to devour greedily
2. to scale a height
3. To have sexual intercourse
4. to bring to completion

See Appendix II for answers.

*Jargon:*

I lay no blame at the door of someone whose speech is confused because of ignorance, or because he is not quite right in the head. But there is no excuse whatever for one who lathers about in jargon, whether he is motivated by pomposity, mental torpidity, or uncertainty. Jargon is a farrago of long, abstract words, curious suffixes, and sentences in the passive voice. It does not have the excuse of being a true code language, though it is frequently employed among peers, so effectively that it may be meaningless not only to outsiders but to the peers themselves. I treasure this extract from a school publication:

> Totally obsolete teaching methods based on imprinting concepts instead of growthful actualizing of potential have created the intellectual ghetto. If schools would stop labeling cooperation "cheating," and adopt newer methods of student interaction, we wouldn't keep churning out these competitive isolates.

In this case, there is no question about the meaning. The writer wanted to say "Let the kids cheat," but did not quite dare say it flatly. Often, though, jargon is impenetrable—and, I have no doubt, intentionally so. It is subject to interpretation according to desire, like the messages of the Delphic oracle: no matter what happens, the jargoneer can say that if you had any sense, you would have known that was exactly what he meant. Such jargoneers remind me of an obstetrician who functioned with great success in the days before it was possible to predict accurately the sex of an unborn child. If an expectant mother asked him to perform that impossibility, he would say firmly, "Boy!" (or "girl!" if that was what he thought she wanted). Then he would add: "And just to show you how sure I am, I am writing my prediction down on this pad, and putting it away in my drawer for you to have as a souvenir after the baby is born." He naturally wrote the opposite of what he had said, knowing that if his oral guess was right the mother would never ask for the paper, while if he had guessed wrong he had proof that she had misheard him.

Perhaps the most widely ridiculed jargon is governmentese, or bureaucratese, far too firmly implanted to be uprooted by the feeble tugs of Bill Safires, Ed Newmans, and Ted Bernsteins. The Senate Finance Committee, for instance, voted to extend a 10 per cent investment tax credit to "unitary hog-raising facilities," known more commonly as pigpens. Governmentese includes expressions like "parameters," "variables," "context," "input," "taken under advisement," "position statements," "finalized," "printouts," "terminal objectives," "visual surveillance," "game plans," "short falls," and "cost overruns." On the other hand, President Carter's statement that "I, along with the people of our country, are tired of seeing the taxpayer's money wasted" is not governmentese, or any other kind of jargon; it is simply bad grammar.

Perhaps the worst offenders of all, and certainly the ones who should know better, are teachers and, especially, professors. I have heard professors of English who sounded as if they were professors of Russian. Or, indeed, any language—except English.

As to the sociologists, economists, and other expositors of arcane half-knowledge—don't talk. John Kenneth Galbraith, a witty and cogent purveyor of spoken and written English, explains the jargon of his fellow economists as follows:

> Complexity and obscurity have professional value—they are the academic equivalents of apprenticeship rules in the building trades. They exclude the outsiders, keep down the competition, preserve the image of a privileged or priestly class. The man who makes things clear is a scab. He is criticized less for his clarity than his treachery.

Dr. Galbraith is over-kind. Jargon generally reflects unclear or incomplete thought. It is impossible to be wholly clear about something you do not really understand. I discovered this years back when *Fortune* magazine asked me to explain for its readers the famous Phase Theory developed by Yale's Professor Willard Gibbs. The theory, which revolutionized modern industry, was over my head. As a result my article was jargon, and the editor defenestrated it. Many jargoneers, however, lack my excuse of ignorance; they have deliberately directed their minds into verbal quicksand. They appear, I told the Hermit Hoar, to take pleasure in death by suffocation.

"Then suffocation is too good an end for them," said the Hermit Hoar. "We need a law making the penalty for jargon automatic disembowelment, to be topped off by beheading."

I would pass on this idea to my congressman, were it not that by reason of his job he would be honor-bound to write the bill in jargon.

# EIGHT

## SESQUIPEDALIA

THERE is a lake in south-central Massachusetts," I told the Hermit Hoar, "that once had the longest place name in the United States. I can't pronounce it, but I can write it out for you."

And I did:

CHARGOGGAGOGGMANCHAUGGAGOGGCHAUBUNA QWNGAMANNG.

"What does it mean?" asked the Hermit Hoar.

"It is Indian for 'You fish on your side of the lake I fish on my side of the lake nobody fish in the middle.'"

"Admirably sesquipedalian," said the Hermit Hoar. "Let me give you a word that is hippopotomonstrosesquipedalian. It is from the Greek, and has 176 letters. Allow me a little time to arrange them in order."

He wrote carefully on the side margin of an old newspaper, using an indelible pencil which he occasionally licked, leaving a purple stain on his thin lips. At length he handed me the newspaper, and shuffled to the well to dredge up beer. The word was:

LOPADOTEMACHOSELACHOGALEOKRANIOLEIPSAN ODRIMHYPOTRIMMATOSILPHIOPARAOMELITOKAT AKECHYMENOKICHLEPIKOSSYPHOPHATTOPERISTT

## ERALEKTRYONOPTEKEPHALLIOKIGKLOPELEIOLAG OIOSIRAIOBAPHETRAGANOPTERYGON.

"And what does that mean?"

"Roughly, 'A goulash composed of all the leftovers from the meals of the leftovers from the meals of the last two weeks.' Aristophanes. *The Ecclesiazusae.*"

"I have a feeling that I used that word in one of my books," I said. "Maybe two. I have been known to repeat myself."

"Quite," said the Hermit Hoar.

"But still—176 letters just to say 'hash'!"

"Quite," he said again. "If you mean hash, say hash—unless you are trying to be funny. And only then if you are Aristophanes."

"Dmitri Borgmann has a chemical term of 1,185 letters in his book *Beyond Language,*" I said, "and I believe I have seen words longer than that."

"Words of a hundred or more letters are not uncommon in some languages," said the Hermit Hoar. "Welsh, German, and Hawaiian, for instance."

"An unusually long word can be amusing, even as part of conversation. Double-dactyl verses cry out to be read aloud, even though the form demands that one of the lines consist of a giant six-syllable word."

"Quite," said the Hermit Hoar for the third time. He refilled our beers. "They are a twentieth-century invention by three men named, if memory serves, Hecht, Hollander, and Pascal. Have you ever written a double-dactyl?"

"Several," I said, "but I don't seem to have the knack. My last one was a tribute to Hecht, Hollander, and Pascal. Or maybe a challenge."

"Can you remember it?" asked the Hermit Hoar.

"I can. It went like this:

Dribble a scribble a
Hecht on you Hollander
Pascal vobiscum you
Lyrical three!

Write me a poem in
Proceleusmaticus;
Then I'll concede you are
Better than me!"

"What is proceleusmaticus?" asked the Hermit Hoar.

"Proceleusmatic, really," I said. "I threw in the -us because I needed the extra syllable. A proceleusmatic is a Greek metric foot of four short syllables. I should think it would be impractical in English."

"So what did you do with your double-dactyl?"

"I entered it in a double-dactyl contest that Emmett Watson was running in the Seattle *Post-Intelligencer.*"

"Did it win?"

"No. He didn't even print it."

The Hermit Hoar nodded in satisfaction. "One more proof," he said, "that you can't fool all the people all the time."

"Wait," I said. "It occurred to me that if there can be a single-word line in a double-dactyl, there is no reason not to make the same arrangement in a limerick."

"One moment, lad," said the Hermit Hoar. "I see the end of the road you are traveling, and I don't like it. I have told you repeatedly, and you have pretended to agree with me, that out of simple courtesy one does not throw into conversation a word unfamiliar to one's companions. It only stigmatizes one as a show-off."

"Except," I said, "when your group happens to be engaged in a rough-and-tumble bout of wordplay. Then anything goes. Would you like some examples?"

The Hermit Hoar shrugged and poured beer. I recited:

**CYPRIPAREUNIAPHILES** (SĬP-ri-pār-O͞ON-i-ə-fīles)

Said a hooker who works out of Niles,
"Cypripareuniaphiles
  Are easy to please—
  They'll pay for a squeeze,
And double for pinches or smiles."

"You will forgive me," said the Hermit Hoar, "for being unfamiliar with the term cypripareuniaphile."

"A cypripareuniaphile," I said, "is one who takes special pleasure in sexual intercourse with prostitutes. Then there are the acynaoblepsianites:

**ACYNAOBLEPSIANITES** (a-SĒN-ə-o-BLEP-sē-ə-nīts)

Acynaoblepsianites
Know yellows from greens, pinks, and whites.
  But blues for such folks
  Are just off-color jokes,
Or songs wailed on sorrowful nights."

"An acynaoblepsianite, I take it, being one who cannot distinguish the color blue."

"You are right," I said, feeling somewhat let down. "Now, returning to prostitutes—"

"You are forever returning to prostitutes," said the Hermit Hoar disapprovingly.

"Only for purposes of rhyme," I said. "Listen closely:"

**ACHLOROPHYLLACEIOUSNESS** (a-KLŎR-ō-fĭl-ā-sē-ŭs-nes)

A whore said, "I couldn't care less
If my john's black or white, but confess
  I'd feel rather nervous
  If called on to service
Achlorophyllaceiousness."

"The joke is off-color," said the Hermit Hoar. "And the word means complete lack of color."

"A true friend," I said, "would not take such pleasure in always trumping my ace. All right—one last limerick. An easy word this time.

**PREANTEPENULTIMATELY** (prē-ĂN-tĭ-pə-NŬL-tĭ-mət-lē)

The faults you complain of in me
Are the sap of my family tree.
  They sprang from the loins
  Of great-granddaddy Boynes . . .
Preantepenultimately."

"Third from the last, your great-grandfather being three generations back," said the Hermit Hoar. "Enough of this nonsense. Your book should emphasize little words, not big ones."

*Words with One Syllable:*

"It will," I said, thumbing through my manuscript. And I read this contribution by Robert T. Harker, called "What is the word in the blank?":

> It has been my lot to have read through scores of proofs each year and one strange fact stands out. Most of those who wish to be seers clothe their thoughts in words which are so long and vague that they do not make sense. Thus the torch passed on to us, which should burn with a bright flame, is but dim and dull, and we are left to grope in the murk. The time spent to get scripts and proofs fit for press must cost a fair sum of hard cash and must raise a book's price in the long run.

The Book of Books, which has no peer, points out the true way of life in word and phrase so brief and clear that "men, though fools, shall not err." Could we not in our own small way do the same? It is true that some terms, such as the names of drugs, can be long, but this does not mean that each word must match them in length. It may be thought that fresh facts cannot be put over in this terse way. If you have read this far and it has made some sort of sense, I would point out that this is not much of a feat: each word save the last is ————.

"So why did you stop reading?" asked the Hermit Hoar.

"You are supposed to supply the last word," I said.

" 'Unisyllabic,' of course," said the Hermit Hoar impatiently.

Certainly one should not use two syllables where one will do, and so on up the line. But what a dull language it would be if all words had only one syllable! Even in speech, we need a mix— words that can hide under a leaf, and words that shadow the earth with their pinions. At the next dinner party I attend, I propose to turn to the woman beside me and say, "What a charming creature you are! Would you like to spend next weekend with me at my place on Lake Chargoggagoggmanchauggagoggchaubunaqwngamanng?"

# NINE

## PRONUNCIATION, WITH ½ TBSP. SPELLING

$A$T great intervals the Hermit Hoar pays me a visit. Since usually he leaves his rocking chair only for his outhouse or the beer well, it surprises me that he can traverse the swamp, climb the huckleberry hill, pick his way through the gorse this side, and arrive at my cottage unwinded.

This day he wished to check certain debatable pronunciations in the five dictionaries I keep on hand for my work. We found that each of the pronunciations below was approved by at least two of the five dictionaries:

- Dour. DŎOR, DOWR.
- Culinary. KYO͞O-lə-nĕ-rē, CUL-i-nĕ-rē.
- Precedence. PRĔS-ə-dəns, PRĒ-cə-dəncE, pri-SĒD-əns.
- Genealogy. jĕn-ē-AL-ə-jē, jē-nē-ĂL-ə-je, JĒ-nē-AWL-ə-je.
- Incognito. ĭn-KŎG-nə-tō, ĭn-kŏg-NĒ-tō.
- Grimace. Gri-MĀS, GRĬM-is.
- Inexplicable. ĭn-ĔK-splĭ-kə-bəl, ĭn-ĭk-SPLĬK-ə-bəl.
- Lamentable. LĂM-ən-tə-bəl, lə-MEN-tə-bəl.
- Schism. SĬZ-əm, SKĬZ-əm.
- Mineralogy. mĭn-ər-ĂL-ə-je, Mĭn-ər-ŎL-ə-jē.
- Secretive. sĕ-KRĒT-ĭv, SĒ-krə-tĭv.

· Domicile. DŎM-ə-sīl, DŌM-ə-sĭl, DŌM-ə-sīl.
· Vagary. və-GĀ-rē, VĀ-gə-rē.

In the above cases, my own preferred pronunciation is the one first listed. But bless you, if you prefer another, and can find some dictionary to back you, say it your way.

I have no self-replenishing jug of beer, but I did place a bottle opener and several bottles of a brand called Olympia on the stand beside Uncle Allie's old chair. (I never use the chair myself; it bothers Author Unknown for me to sit there.) I also threw another alder log on the fire.

"Never underestimate the power of pronunciation," began the Hermit Hoar. "Poor pronunciation was killing men as far back as Old Testament times. When the Gileadites were fighting the Ephraimites, they would demand of a captured suspect—where is your Bible, my lad? Ah, yes—'Art thou an Ephraimite? If he said, Nay, Then said they unto him, Say now Shibboleth*; and he said Sibboleth; for he could not frame to pronounce it right. Then they took him, and slew him.' "†

I said, "When the Sicilians were trying to drive out the French, they made suspects say *Cicero ce-ci,* pronounced Chichero Chechi."

"Cicero chick-peas," said the Hermit Hoar.

"Yes. Four 'ch' sounds are required in rapid succession. The French would turn 'ch' into 'sh,' and were shot out of hand."

"In World War II, Japanese pretending to be Filipinos were ordered to say 'lollapaloosa.' They could not say 'l'; they said 'r' instead. Anyone who said 'Raraparooza' did not last long."

"Then I may be in deeper trouble than I had realized," I said. "All my life I have been pronouncing 'conduit' as if it had three syllables: 'KON-dōo-it,' or, at best, 'KOND-wit.' Recently I looked up the word, and one of the syllables had vanished. ' "KON-dĭt" or "KUN-dĭt," ' said the dictionaries. They all agreed. No 'KON-dōo-ĭt' at all."

"You should have looked longer," said the Hermit Hoar. "Webster's accepts the third syllable. It has to be accepted. When enough educated people adopt a pronunciation, the dictionaries have to give in."

"Considering the jumble of our backgrounds," I mused, "it is no wonder that Americans disagree occasionally on pronunciation, not to mention usage. The wonder is that we can understand each other at all."

"I blame snobbery; you blame pioneer intermingling," said the Hermit Hoar. "In any event, English has a wonderful way of shap-

* *Shibboleth* means literally an ear of corn, or a stream, or a flood.
† Judges 12:5–6.

ing words to its own ends. We may keep the sound when we adopt a foreign word, but more often we anglicize it—French *route du roi*‡ to 'Rotten Row,' Dutch *nit wiet*\* to *'nitwit.'* I pronounce val-et 'val-LAY,' you say 'VAL-et.' Who's right? We both are. There are many ways to be wrong in English, but it is a comfort to know there are also many ways to be right."

He was thumbing through Leon Edel's *Henry James*. "There was more rigidity a few years back," he said. "Listen to this anecdote about old Henry":

> In later years Rosina (Emmet—a young cousin of James) was to relate how on one of their walks together, Henry James, with much affection and yet a kind of merciless regularity, kept her attention fixed on the sound of her own voice. Hoping to engage him in conversation, she had commented on how charming she found the jewel in his tie-pin.
>
> "Jew-*el*, not j*ool*," her Distinguished Cousin rejoined, ignoring the compliment.
>
> "I'm afraid American girls don't speak their vowels distinctly," Rosina ventured.
>
> "Vow-*el* not v*owl*, Rosina."
>
> Tears came. "Oh, Cousin Henry, you are so cruel!"
>
> "Cru-*el* not cr*ool*, Rosina."
>
> And the youngest cousin Leslie remembered that when she said, "I must go upstairs and fix my hair," Cousin Henry looked at her fixedly, and then said solemnly:
>
> "To fix your hair, my dear Leslie? To *fix* it to what—and with what?"

"Our problem is not just slovenliness of tongue, is it?" I asked. "In reading, most of us understand as a matter of course words we may not pronounce or hear spoken a dozen times in our lives. How can we expect to be right every time we speak?"

"Well, there *are* rules. As we were just saying, many words have at least two acceptable pronunciations. If a man knows them both, but prefers a variant of his own, isn't that his right?"

"If he does not mind being laughed at."

"The fact," said the Hermit Hoar, "that Lord Kennet was perfectly aware of the correct pronunciation of 'phalarope' did not prevent him from writing:

I live in hope some day to see
The crimson-necked phal-Ā-rō-pē;
(Or, do I, rather, live in hope
To see the red-necked phal-a-RŌP?"

‡ The king's road. But some say the present name comes from the onetime prevalence of horse droppings.
\* "I don't understand."

"Which is right?"

"Phal-a-RŌP. Unless one likes phal-Ā-rō-pē better. It is a small shore bird, by the way, something like a sandpiper. The female does the courting."

"An interesting twist. Kennet might have added something like,

When stubborn maids say, 'No, you dope!'
I wish I were a phalarope."

"Lord Kennet lacked your morbid preoccupations," said the Hermit Hoar. "Besides, he would never have uttered a word like 'dope.'"

"It must be a puzzlement to foreigners," I said, "that a single combination of letters may make so many sounds in English. 'Ough' must be the best-known example. It is pronounced at least five ways—maybe six; I have a feeling there is an 'ug' sound in there somewhere."

The Hermit Hoar began to count on his fingers. "There is 'oo,' he said; there is 'ow'—"

I interrupted. "You knew Arthur Clough, the Victorian poet, I think?"

"Of course. A melancholy sort; always worrying about God."

"I brought together the five 'ough' sounds I could remember in an appreciation of him," I said. "Listen:

### ON ARTHUR CLOUGH, A VICTORIAN POET

I seldom rest beneath a bough
To read the lines of Arthur Clough.
I find his thoughts insipid, though
Victorians loved Arthur Clough.
Indeed, they could not get enough
Of platitudes by Arthur Clough.
I groan, I gulp, I snort, I cough
When I must wade through Arthur Clough;
And I am glad that I am through
With this review of Arthur Clough."

"Spoken and written English are two different languages," said the Hermit Hoar. "Some 80 per cent of our words are not spelled the way they sound. It's a fact; I have it from Richard Lederer, the logologist. It is impossible to pronounce any word, even cat, simply by looking at it; you have to be told first. The e's in 're-entered,' for instance, have four different pronunciations, including one silent letter. In 'though,' 'gh' lacks all sound; in 'ghoul' it is a hard 'g'; in 'hiccough,' a 'p'; and in 'rough,' an 'f.' George Bernard Shaw pointed out that by pronouncing 'gh' as in 'tough,' 'o' as in 'women,' and 'ti' as in 'motion,' one derives 'fish' from 'ghoti.' Pronounce 'c' as in 'cue,' 'e' as in 'eye,' 'a' as in 'are,' 's' as in 'sea,' and 'e' as in 'ell': 'cease' becomes 'quircl.' "

I said, "George Starbuck wrote a caudated sonnet that rhymed fifteen words with 'owe'—and every word ended in a different letter. I have it in one of my books. Writing," I said, "is much safer than talking."

"Quite," said the Hermit Hoar. "When you write, you can hide behind your words. When you talk, you are up front, like the clown in the midway booth; any passer-by can bean you with a ball."

"An apt, if colloquial, analogy," said I. "An author named Jerzy Kosinski made the same point well—"

"Better than I did?" asked the Hermit Hoar in an offended tone.

"Differently, that's all. He was chatting with Delfina Rattazzi— you have not met her, I think; she is a book editor of Italian background, in New York. Kosinski told her, 'Write. When you write, you don't have an accent.' "

"But why should she worry about an accent?" asked the Hermit Hoar in purest Oxonian. "All Americans have accents."

*Lazy pronunciation:*

While I am willing to shut my ears to certain heterodox pronunciations, my tolerance does not extend to the sort that result from simple dullness of ear and laziness of tongue. New York's station WBAI-FM, for instance, recently presented a marathon reading of Tolstoi's *War and Peace*. Richard E. Harrison, the cartographer, found his mind wandering from the story to the blurred articulations of the volunteers who did the reading. Here is some of the sloppy speech he jotted down:

For irrelevant, irrevelant; for observation, asseration; for dissipated, dessipated; for heterogeneous, heterogenous; for valet, wallet; for stout, stoot; for alacrity, alicrity; for magnanimity, magnaminity; for rapidity, rapidy; for *War and Peace, Warn Peace* (many times); for occasionally, occasionly; for advantageous, adventatious; for stealthily, stethily.

It took 119 readers to present the entire book. When No. 12 read "a phenomenon" as "a phenomena," Mr. Harrison sighed, shut off the set, and went back to making maps.

Some northeastern barbarisms should have been cited earlier. Particularly prevalent is the transposition of "t" or "th" into "d"; "de" for "the," "dat" for "that," "ledder" for "letter," "badder" for "batter," "thirdy" for "thirty." "Utter" and "other" both come out "udder"—a word, according to speech pundit Dorothy Sarnoff, that should be reserved for the pendant mammary gland. Here is how not to pronounce "smarty," "party," "McCarthy," "another," "brother":

## SMARDY, SMARDY

Smardy, smardy, had a pardy;
No one came but Joe McCardy;
Smardy, smardy, had anudder;
No one came but Smardy's brudder.

In the Northeast, too, tongue laziness sometimes works backward. Many New Yorkers call Long Island "Long GI-land." Precedent is on their side; we call England "ING-gland," don't we?

Here is the sort of lazy tonguemanship that discouraged Ricky Harrison:

## DON'T KNOW

When I speak, do faces shine
At my fine melodic line?
Do men ape in admiration
My precise pronunciation?
  Oh . . .
  I dunno.

## LET ME, GIVE ME

I offered Emmy
  Whiskey plain.
She said, "Lemme
  Have champagne."
I offered Jimmy
  Whiskey neat.
He said, "Gimme
  Aquavit."

## BECAUSE

I met a man
Astride a hoss;
He said, "I ride
This hoss becawss"
(Or else perhaps
He said "becuz";
I can't recall
Which way it was)

"I'm tolt
This colt
Won't bolt."

## WANT TO

Your iguana, I can tell,
Does not know the language well.
Your iguana
Says, "I wanna."

## DID YOU

Slap like a midge a
Man who says "didja."

## STRENGTH

Sir Galahad was strong as ten.
He said, "My pure heart lends me strenth."
("Length" may also turn to "lenth.")
His accent's something else again:
Its strenth is nearer to a tenth.

## HEIGHT

For "height," you keep on saying "heighth."
I might not hit you, but I mighth.

## WIDTH, FIFTH, OFTEN

Your "width" sounds very much like "with";
Your "fifth" sounds very much like "fith";
And please, can't you soften
Your "off-ten" to "often"?

*Spelling:*
I would ignore spelling entirely in these remarks, except that some words cannot be located in the dictionary unless they are spelled right. A professor of English named Josef Fox asked his Humanities class at an Iowa college to write their views on the bourgeoisie. Three fourths of the students could not even spell the name. Some of their approximations: Beorgeoisie, bourgeous, boursgioese, bourgusie, bourgeousis, bourgeusie, boursegeise, bourgeiouses, boureiese, bourgoissie, bourgesie, bourgeseau, bourgeosle, bourg, bougeoswle, beorsolse, bourgsosie, bourgouse, bour-

geise, boureogisie, burgousise, bourgeouise, bouregouies, boushazze, bourgesois, bougeousie, bourgeosise, bourgeoisee, bouisyase, burgeouisie, burgeouisie, bourguiesie, bourgeasie, bourgugesie, burgoeise, burgosie, bourgesie, burgoeise, bourgosie, bourgesie, burgeoise, bourgosie, bourgoisie, boeusgouis, bourguiouise, bougoise, bougeoisie, bourgeouisee, bourouise, bourgiese, bourgeoise, bourzwarzie, boursousie, bourgeausie, bourgeousie, bourgoisie, bourgeieose, bourgeiose, borgouse, bourgouise, boursies, bourgiousie, bourguise, bourgousies, borageosis, burgious, burogios, bourgose, boursgousis, bourgeosies, bourgeosis, bouregosis, bourguesie, bourgoreise, bourouguise, bougousie, bourgenoise, beurgoisse, burgeoise, bourgoisse, burgeuse, bourgeseise, burgoisie, burgeoisie.

Dr. Lawrence Whitcomb of Lehigh University found seventeen misspellings of "Appalachian" in ninety-two examination papers: Appleacheean, Appalactions, Applacians, Appalechins, Appulation, Appelation, Appalechin, Aplachian, Applachian, Appilation, Appliachian, Applachant, Application, Applachain, Apalatian, Applacachin, Apalachian.

That teachers themselves are not immune to poisoned spelling is indicated in this UPI dispatch from Lafayette, Louisiana:

> A teacher who moved to Louisiana from Texas pointed out to the local newspaper that the school board pays substitute teachers only $25 a day. "What does the board expect to get for this kind of pay?" She asked.
>
> The one-paragraph letter contained seven errors in grammar and spelling, including two misspellings of the word substitute.

The picket sign of a striking teacher carried this legend:

> "On strike for a descent wage."

If you cannot help misspelling, I suggest you turn your failing into an amusement, as Mr. Anonymous did here:

### THE PTARMIGAN

The Ptarmigan is pterrible,
  Ill-ptempered as can be;
He ptarries not on ptelephone poles,
  Nor ptumbles from a ptree,
And the way he ptakes to spelling
  Is a ptiresome thing pto me.

I hav nothing more to say about speling.

*Words Often Mispronounced:*

I mentioned earlier, or at least I meant to, that in pronunciation one man's meat may be another man's poison. All I can say for my own preferences is that they are shared by a number of presumably educated Americans. The following list of preferred pronunciations was prepared in 1905 by Sherwin Cody, and has been somewhat modernized. You need not agree with all his choices; but if you agree with most of them, your pronunciation will be superior to that of most of your friends. Vowels are short unless otherwise indicated. The phonetic symbols are Mr. Cody's.

Accent. ac-CENT a word, but give the word an AC-cent.

Acclimate. ac-CLĪM-ate.

Accurate. ak-KŪ, not ak-ER.

Acoustics. a-KOO, not a-KOW.

Advertisement. accent VER rather than tise.

Again. en in U.S.; ān in England.

Against. genst.

Aged. an Ā-ged person, two syllables; properly āged, one syllable.

Albumen. accent *bu*, not *al*.

Algebra. not brā.

Alias. ĀL-yus, not a-LĪ-as.

Alien. yen, not i-en.

Almond. l silent, AH-mund.

Apricot. Ā-pricot.

Arab. arab, not ārab.

Archangel. ark, not arch.

Arkansas. by law, AR-kan-saw.

Asia. Ā-zhe-a, not Ā-zha.

Askance. as-CANS, not ASK-ans.

Audacious. dā, not dash.

Awkward. ward, not ard; sound the w.

Ay or aye (yes). ī.

Bade. băd, not bād.

Been. bin in U.S.; bēn in England.

Bicycle. accent bī, y short.

Biennial. long i in bi.

Biography. long i in bi.

Blackguard. BLAG-gard.

Blatant. blā.

Blessed. the BLESS-ed, two syllables; he was blessed, one syllable.

Bowsprit. bō, not bow.

Breeches. BRICH-ez.

Brooch. brōch.

Brougham. broom.

Business. BIZ-ness.

Caldron. cawl, not cal.

Calk. kawk, not kawlk.

Carbine. bīn, not bin.

Carousel. roo, not row.

Cement. accent either syllable for noun, last syllable for verb.

Chasten. chās, not chas; t silent.

Chastisement. accent chas, not tise.

Chestnut. t silent.

Chic. shēk, not shik or chik.

Chicanery. i is short, accent cā.

Civilization. i before z is not long.

Cleanly. He is a cleanly (klen) person; he does his work cleanly (kleen).

Cognac. KŌN-yak.

Column. um, not yum.

Compatriot. pā, not pat.

Conduit. CON-dit or CUN-dit.

Conjure. I con-JURE you; he could CUN-jure like a magician.

Conquest. kong, not kon.

Contrast. It is a good CON-trast; the colors con-TRAST well.

Conversant. accent con.

Converse. He con-VERSED well; I can prove the CON-verse.

Convoy. They con-VOYED the CON-voy.

Coupon. coo, not cū.

Courtier. KŌRT-yer.

Creek. not krik.

Cupboard. cub.

Cynosure. accent cy, long y.

Deaf. def, not dēf.

Decade. accent dec.

Decisive. cī, not cis.

Definitive. accent fin.

Desert. the DES-ert; his de-SERTS; we de-SERT.

Despicable. accent des.

Dessert. accent zert.

Dilemma. short i, accent lem.

Directly. short i.

Disputant. accent dis.

Docile. dos, not dō.

Dolorous. dol, not dōl.

Douche. doosh.

Drought. drowt.

Ecce Homo. EK-se HŌ-mō.

Err. rhymes with were.

Every. EV-e-ry, three syllables.

Exigency. accent ex.

Exquisite. accent ex.

Extant. accent tant.

Extraordinary. tror.

Falcon. faw, not fal.

Familiarity. yar, not i-ar.

Feminine. nin, not nīn.

Finale. fi-NAH-le, short i.

Forbade. bad, not bād.

Formidable. accent for.

Frequent. It was a FRE-quent occurrence; we fre-QUENT-ed the hall.

Gallant. He was GAL-lant on the field, and gal-LANT in the parlor.

Genial. yal (preferred) rather than i-al.

Glisten. t silent.

God. not gawd.

Gooseberry. gooz, not goos.

Granary. gran, not grān.

Handkerchief. hang-ker-chif.

Hearth. harth, not herth.

Heinous. HĀ-nus.

Herb. the h is silent.

Heroine. her, soft e, not hē.

Hiatus. hī-Ā-tus.

Hoop. like loop.

Hospitable. accent hos.

Hover. huv, not hov.

Hygienic. hī-gi-EN-ic.

Hypocrisy. first y short.

Illustrate. accent lus.

Impious. IM-pi-ous, not im-pī-ous.

Implacable. plā.

Importune. accent tune.

Imprimatur. accent mā.

Inaugurate. au-gū, not au-ger.

Incomparable. accent com.

Incorporeal. accent pō.

Increase. Count the IN-crease; the sum in-CREAS-es.

Indisputable. accent dis.

Industry. accent in.

Inexpiable. accent ex.

Inexplicable. accent ex.

Ingenious. yus (preferred), not i-us.

Inhospitable. accent hos.

Inquiry. accent quī.

Instinct. My IN-stinct tells me I am in-STINCT with life.

Interest. IN-ter-est, three syllables.

Intestine. tin, not tīn.

Intrigue. accent trigue.

Inveigle. vē.

Italic. first i short.

Lamentable. accent lam.

Lang syne. sīn, not zīn.

Learned. If I had LEARN-d more, I would be more LEARN-ed.

Lettuce. tis, not tus.

Levee. LEV-ee, bank of river; lev-ĒĒ, gathering of guests.

Literature. choor or tūr.

Long-lived. long i, not as in *to live*.

Lyceum. accent ce.

Mischievous. MIS-chiv-us, not mis-CHĒV-i-us.

Moisten. t silent.

Molecule. mol; but mō-LEC-u-lar.

Naked. nā, not neck.

Obeisance. bā or bē, accented; the i does not sound.

Obelisk. ob, not ōb.

Obscenity. sen, not sēn.

Occult. accent cult.

Office. not awfus.

Often. t silent.

Omelet. OM-e-let, three syllables.

Pall Mall. pell mell.

Parent. pār, not par.

Patriot. pā.

Perspiration. not pres.

Phonics. fōn, not fon.

Poignant. g silent.

Precedent. He had a prē-CĒ-dent position, but it did not form a PREC-e-dent.

Predecessor. pred, not prēd.

Predilection. prē (preferred)

Prelate. prel.

Premature. prē.

Presentation. prez.

Pretense. accent tense.

Pretty. prit, not purt.

Probity. prob, not prŏb.

Process. pro in U.S.; prō in England.

Project. He is prō-JECT-ing a new PROJ-ect.

Pseudonym. p silent.

Puerile. il, not īl.

Purport. accent pur.

Quay. kē.

Rapine. rap, not răp.

Ration. răsh, not rash.

Really. rē-al-ly, three syllables.

Record. Rē-CORD his name in this REC-erd.

Refutable. accent fūt.

Reparable. accent rep.

Research. accent search.

Resource. accent source.

Respite. pit, not pīt; accent on first syllable.

Resplendent. rē, not re.

Resume. I will rē-SUME work on my re-zu-MĀ.

Revocable. accent rev.

Robust. accent the bust, not the rōbe.

Root. rhymes with boot.

† See page 169 for schwa pronunciation.

Sacrilegious. LĒ-jus, not LI-jus.

Satiety. accent tī, not sā.

Saucy. saws, not sas.

Schism. ch silent, SIZ-əm.†

Senile. sēn, not sen.

Sentient. SEN-she-ent.

Short-lived. līvd, not livd.

Sinecure. sīn, not sin.

Sleek. not slick.

Soften. t silent.

Solecism. sol, not sōl.

Subtile (fine, thin). SUB-til.

Subtle (artful). SUT-l, b silent.

Suite. swēt, not sūt.

Surprise. not sup.

Survey. I sur-VEY; I make a SUR-vey.

Syringe. accent syr.

Teat. not tit.

Ticklish. TIK-lish, two syllables; not TIK-el-ish.

Tirade. accent rād.

Toward. w silent.

Tribune. trib, not trīb.

Valuable. VAL-u-a-ble, four syllables; not VAL-u-ble.

Vehemence. accent ve.

Velvet. not vit.

Villain. VIL-lin, not lun.

Which. not wich.

While. not wile.

Wont (no apostrophe). wunt.

# TEN

## VOCABULARY

### IN YUPIK

"In Yupik, there are forty-seven words for a walrus, depending on what he's doing. There is no word for time. You tell me who's got the proper values."

—Clay Hardy
U. S. Fish and Wildlife Service

SINCE the eighteenth century, when Dr. Johnson met the Hermit Hoar, English has gained hundreds of thousands of words, and lost a few. In Johnson's day, the Hermit Hoar's conversation was studded with the likes of adversable, advesperate, adjugate, agriculation, abstrude, spicocity, morigerous, balbucinate, and illachrymable. Occasionally he still says injudicable, crapulence, and tenebrosity, but I do not consider these words obsolete; if they no longer have a place in the language, they should have.

In general, though, the Hermit Hoar speaks now like any other person of reasonable education, British or American.

So when he says he thinks we Americans sometimes try to enlarge our accumulation of spoken words past the bounds of common sense, I listen to him with respect.

He was appalled when I mentioned the other day a survey showing that the average college sophomore knows two hundred thousand words.*

"Two hundred thou—" The Hermit Hoar choked on his beer, sending barm flying about the solemn cell. "Bless my soul! What college sophomores are those?"

"The study," I said, "was made at the Alabama Institute of Technology."

* Professor George W. Hartman, Columbia University, study reported in *Word Power Made Easy*, by Norman Lewis.

"Bless my soul!" he repeated, shaking his head. "Alabama, of all places! What do they do with all those words?"

"They communicate."

"No one needs two hundred thousand words just to *communicate*," said the Hermit Hoar. "A sophomore, especially, needs only someone to communicate *with*. Of the opposite sex, if possible."

"You sound like Christine, my mother-in-law's maid. She spoke only Rumanian. She fell in love with the handyman, who spoke only Greek, and they married. After the honeymoon, my mother-in-law congratulated Christine on appearing so happy when she and her husband had no common language. She asked how they could talk and Christine replied, *'Pentruce atâta vorbă?'* In English: 'What's so much to talk about?'"

"Your mother-in-law's maid was an intelligent woman."

"Hermit Hoar," I asked curiously, "what do you consider an adequate speaking vocabulary?"

"Oh—just for starters, of course—say 850 words."

It was my turn to choke on my beer.

"I said 'for starters.' Of course words have to be added for specialized areas. But basic English consists of 850 words, and pidgin is about the same. Juggle the words properly, and there is little of a nontechnical nature they cannot communicate. How large do you suppose Chaucer's vocabulary was?"

"I have no idea."

"I have; I taught him most of it. He used roughly 8,000 words, counting the compounds. The King James Bible required fewer than 6,000, and Milton fewer than 11,000. Shakespeare used around 20,000."

"But there are more than a million identifiable and accepted English words."

"I know—the accretion, largely, of our specialized, technological civilization. An average adult, though, has a use-and-recognition vocabulary of no more than 30,000 to 60,000 words. A highly literate man or woman may recognize 100,000. I assume you see what that means?"

I again confessed ignorance.

"It means that even if you are well educated and cosmopolitan in your interests, nine tenths of the words in English are meaningless to you. To all intents and purposes, they are a foreign language."

"Then what is the use of those other 900,000 words?"

"They are there for the specialists. Outside their specialities, even specialists commonly speak within a range of about 20,000 words. A quarter of our entire conversation consists of repeating just seventeen words: 'and,' 'be,' 'have,' 'it,' 'of,' 'the,' 'to,' 'will,' 'you,' 'I,' 'a,' 'on,' 'that,' 'in,' 'we,' 'for,' and 'is.' The most common of all are 'I,' 'the,' 'and,' 'to,' 'of,' 'in,' 'we,' 'for,' 'you,' and 'a.'"

"Why not 'me'?"

"I think it should be added."

(The next day I tried to put the 17 most commonly used words as often as I could into a verse. It came out like this):

## WHEN I AM YOU, AND YOU ARE I

When I am you, and you are I,
At what a rate the time will fly!
For what a to-do it will be
When I am you, and you are me!

When you are you, and we are us,
That will, for us, be glorious—
That is, if she and I are her—
Like us, of blameless character.

And on the sly, we'll wed, for we
Are us, not her, or him, or he.
We have to take this rather far:
To tie it in with what we are,
We have a spot of thought to do,
For I am I; and you are you,
*It, be, have, and, of, the, will, to,*
*You, I, a, on—we, for.*
Adieu.

But that was the next day. Now I settled down with my beer to listen.

"Only about 4,000 of the 20,000 words used commonly," the Hermit Hoar was saying, "are of what might be called native English origin. Of the rest, 12,000 are grounded in French, Latin, or Greek. Yet 94 per cent of the words in the Bible, 90 per cent in Shakespeare, 88 per cent in Tennyson, and 81 per cent in Milton are of Anglo-Saxon origin. In speech I suspect the figure would be nearer 95 per cent."

"It is easy to forget," I said, "how much of speech is visual. If you listen to a conversation in the next room, and have never seen the speakers, the chances are nine out of ten that when you walk into the room you will find that you have formed an entirely false impression of both their appearance and their personalities. A good talker makes the most not just of his words and intonations, but his face and body."

"True enough," said the Hermit Hoar. "In some cases the body even takes over most of the job. There are successful and socially popular dancers, tightrope walkers, football players, and the like, who scarcely know any words at all beyond Basic vocabulary, the slang of the moment, and the vocabulary of their trades. At work, their bodies speak for them. Socially, they may be accepted because of their reputations, but they are gimps. They tend to confine their private lives to their own kind, not just because of limited interests but because they can understand and be understood by virtually no one else."

"It is not like you to make such a broad generalization," I said. "I have known athletes who speak the queen's English at least as well as you or I."

(I have always suspected that the Hermit Hoar has been prejudiced against sports in this country ever since we chose baseball instead of cricket as our national game.)

When one is reading, recognition-vocabulary is the key to comprehension. When one is writing, the dictionary and thesaurus are there to lend a hand. But when one is speaking, one is on one's own. The greater the vocabulary that one not only understands on paper but uses as familiarly as "cat" in conversation, the better the conversation, sensitively edited, is likely to be. It is not just a hype that improved speech increases earning power and raises social standing. Though it is currently fashionable in some circles to use outrageous English, just as it is to wear outrageous clothes, the correlation between speech, income, and social status remains constant. The Human Engineering School finds regularly in its surveys that the highest-paid men and women are those who use the language best. We all know exceptions, but the principle is beyond dispute.

The desire to rise in the world is a perfectly valid reason for wishing to increase one's command of spoken English, and for reading this book. But there are other gratifications no less real and compelling, even if they do not present themselves in the form of hand-tailored suits and hundred-foot yachts. Among these is the pleasure of not only knowing what one is talking about, but knowing that one is talking well about it.

If I have ever given you the impression that what you have to say is less important than the way you say it, I have misspoken. What is more pitiable than the person whose vocabulary outstrips his knowledge and comprehension? It is all very well to know that an alder tree is of the genus *Alnus*, but if you cannot tell an alder tree from a birch, your command of the word *Alnus* is not going to help you. If you can recite fifty shades of pink, but cannot tell one from another on sight, your fifty fine names are useless—you are going around with a head full of what Alexander Pope called learned lumber, by which he meant junk. Rather than memorizing the names of plants, go out and weed the garden—*then* check your botany book. Learn by experience to tell sour grass from yellow dock. Unattached words are worthless.

The difference between an exact epithet and an approximation, to plagiarize Mark Twain, is the difference between lightning and the lightning bug. I give you a casual-sounding description by Gerard Durrell of some insects he happened to be watching. Mr. Durrell sees before he writes. Spend the rest of your life trying to match his lucidity:

> In that brilliant, brittle light I could appreciate the true hunts-man's red of a lady-bird's wing case, the magnificent chocolate and amber of an earwig, and the deep shining agate of the ants.

As your vision sharpens, you will know from your own observation the nuance that separates one synonym from another. "Gorse" is one of the rare words that has an exact synonym—"furze." With most identifications, you will not be so lucky. Even an innocuous little word like "wet" is given no less that 148 distinct meanings by the Oxford English Dictionary. Until you can distinguish every one of them from the others, you will not know all that "wet" means. Other words are even more difficult to define, because they sum up not realities but value judgments; "Such words as 'truth' and 'freedom,'" observes Philip Howard, "are so loaded with value judgments that they mean all things to all men."

In your speech, as in your thinking, separate value judgments from facts. You may thus help to save spoken English from the role *Punch* has already assigned it: a handful of phrases, likely to vanish altogether. Frighten yourself by studying *Punch*'s list of the phrases that remain extant. Anyone with a moderate gift for languages, says the English humor magazine, should be able to converse fluently using only the expressions below:

· Actually, in point of fact, well, as a matter of fact, really. = "I am about to say something"

· You know. = "I am halfway through saying something"

· It seems to me, anyway, that's how I see it, as I see it, if you ask me, if you really want to know. = "I have just finished saying something, I think"

· That's what it's all about, isn't it? That's where it's at. There you are, then. That's just it, isn't it? = "I think you're right" (the nearest that Spoken English gets to philosophy)

*N.B. All the above phrases are interchangeable.*

\* \* \*

If you apply the message of this book conscientiously, there is no doubt that you will increase your vocabulary, your earning power, your popularity—perhaps even, if such is your desire, the length of your nose. But don't try to learn all the million words in the language. There is such a thing as having a million drinks too many.

# VERSES TO IMPROVE
# YOUR VOCABULARY

# 1.

## TANDEM, RANDOM, TINGLE-AIRY, HYPOCHONDRIAC, CADGE, AGGRANDIZE

Write your own definition of each key word. Then check the word or phrase you consider nearest in meaning. The correct definitions are in Appendix II.

Let us play at add-a-word
   In the land of faerie;
No word is too bad a word
   For a game so merry.

Words are dancing past your door
   Some abreast, some tandem:
Pick out any three or four,
   Beckon them at random.

Once you beckon, they will stay,
   Though at first they're wary.
Set them in a song, to play
   On your tingle-airy.
      On your tingle-airy . . .

*Hypochondriacs are not*
  *As ill as they imagine;*
*Suits from Savile Row are what*
  *Cadgers often cadge in.*

Words like these will aggrandize
  Your vocabulary.
First, though, try them on for size
  On your tingle-airy.
    On your tingle-airy . . .

Check your preferred definitions below:

TANDEM
1. twins
2. harness horse
3. one behind the other
4. beige

RANDOM
1. carelessness
2. sets of two
3. without a definite pattern
   —haphazard
4. agitation

TINGLE-AIRY
1. folk song
2. wild flower
3. bee hive
4. hand organ

HYPOCHONDRIAC
1. drug addict
2. one neurotically anxious
   over his health
3. deaf person
4. one who uses water
   therapy

CADGE
1. to set traps
2. flatter
3. beg
4. farm tool

AGGRANDIZE
1. irritate
2. inform
3. enlarge
4. succeed

2.

## ATHEIST, ANONYMOUS

An atheist at heaven's gate
  Was ushered in without a fuss:
His membership was up-to-date
  In Atheists Anonymous.

Check your preferred definitions below:

ATHEIST
1. one who says the existence or nonexistence of God is beyond human capacity to judge
2. a believer in God without divine revelation; a freethinker
3. one who denies the existence of God
4. one who believes that God and the universe are identical

ANONYMOUS
1. hidden
2. without a name
3. anarchistic
4. writing under a pseudonym

# 3.

## VIRAGO, BEATITUDE, REPULSIVE, VERBOSE, FARRAGO, VACILLATE (a roundel)

What? Do you in a thumbnail sketch? I may go
Too far, my dear; perhaps I'd kick your shin.
Should I tell all the world you're a virago?
What? Do you in?

You'd have me tell how shamelessly you sin?
Tell my beatitude when you away go?
Say how repulsive is your wrinkled skin?
Your speech verbose, your logic a farrago?
I vacillate . . . Perhaps I should begin . . .
But do you really mean it when you say "Go"?
What? Do you in?

Check your preferred definitions below:

VIRAGO
1. a shrewish woman
2. rheumatism
3. distant star or planet
4. bacteria

BEATITUDE
1. special prayer
2. consummate bliss
3. competition
4. elegance

REPULSIVE
1. pugnacious
2. throbbing
3. recurring
4. repellent or disgusting

| VERBOSE | 1. having more than one meaning |
|---|---|
| | 2. grammatical term |
| | 3. using more words than necessary |
| | 4. loud or offensive |
| FARRAGO | 1. prairie grass |
| | 2. a jumble, mishmash |
| | 3. Spanish dance |
| | 4. gambling game |
| VACILLATE | 1. immunize against |
| | 2. disregard |
| | 3. transpose |
| | 4. fluctuate; waver |

## 4.

### DEBOUCH

In France a fly *s'appelle une mouche*.
    A *mouche* does not cry "Ouch!"
    When swatted it cries "Oosh!"

Reflect now on "debouch":
"The milk debouches from the cow."
    The cow, if hurt, moans "Moo";
    It does not utter "Ow."

Remember this, my friend, when you
    Are rising from your couch;
    Say "I deboosh"
    To rhyme with *oosh*.
    Not "I debouch,"
    To rhyme with ouch.

PREFERRED: DĬ-BOOSH

Check your preferred definition below:
DEBOUCH 1. utter a cry of pain
           2. (verb tr.) to close, as a mouth
           3. to emerge or issue
           4. military—to close ranks

## 5.

### PHILTRUM

I have a little philtrum
Wherein my spilltrum flows

When I am feeling illtrum
And runny at the nose.

Check your preferred definition below:

PHILTRUM  1. eyelid
             2. small bottle
             3. groove on upper lip
             4. a scold

# 6.

## CHARY, LEERY, GUILE, MOTIVATION

I'm chary of the look of you,
    And leery of your guile;
Your motivation's showing through.
And yet your pledges may be true . . .
    I'll hang around awhile.

Check your preferred definitions below:

CHARY      1. two-wheeled carriage
               2. shy, hesitant
               3. red-eyed
               4. avoid

LEERY      1. aware
               2. tipsy
               3. suspicious
               4. animal burrow

GUILE      1. charm
               2. deceitful cunning
               3. veil
               4. armor piece

MOTIVATION  1. expression
               2. creativity
               3. velocity
               4. incentive

# 7.

## GUTTERSNIPE, BIPED, DISDAINFUL, ODIUM, PODIUM

You are just a guttersnipe, Ed—
Just a vulgar human biped,
Treated with disdainful odium

By the preacher from his podium.
(As if *he* were other stripe, Ed,
Than a vulgar human biped.)

Check your preferred definitions below:

GUTTERSNIPE
1. hoarse-voiced person
2. sea bird
3. water crane
4. street Arab or rogue

BIPED
1. having two feet
2. motorcyclist
3. pigeon-toed
4. cattle

DISDAINFUL
1. inattentive
2. laconic
3. at a distance
4. scornful

ODIUM
1. admiration
2. pulpit
3. smell
4. hatred

PODIUM
1. throne
2. microphone
3. dais
4. chrysanthemum

# 8.

## GOURMAND, GOURMET

Said a gourmand to a gourmet,
"Though your appetite is poor, may
I suggest for old time's sake
Each of us should order steak,
Twenty ounces, say, apiece,
Lathered on with axle grease?"

The gourmet did not answer back,
Having died of heart attack.

Check your preferred definitions below:

GOURMAND
1. chef
2. greedy or ravenous eater
3. lecher
4. clown

GOURMET
1. specialist
2. ornament
3. miser
4. a connoisseur of food and drink

# 9.

## ALTRUISTIC, CONCESSION, ARDOR, EXPEDITE, CONCURRENCE, AFTERMATH, OSCULATING

Fairy godma, make her kiss stick!
Somehow it seems altruistic—
More concession to my ardor
Than a hint that I try harder.

Fairy godma, expedite
Her concurrence in my plight!
Let her burn like me, awaiting
Aftermath of osculating!

Check your preferred definitions below:

ALTRUISTIC
1. unselfish
2. independent
3. mountainous
4. honest

CONCESSION
1. recommendation
2. yielding
3. ending
4. arrangement

ARDOR
1. difficult
2. grove of trees
3. fervent affection
4. pantry

EXPEDITE
1. inform
2. travel
3. pedal
4. hasten; quicken

CONCURRENCE
1. a formal cursing; an anathema
2. river current
3. competition, especially in running
4. agreement in opinion or action

AFTERMATH
1. phenomenon
2. delay
3. consequence
4. risk

OSCULATING
1. swinging to and fro
2. kissing
3. leering
4. carousing

# 10.

## DISPARAGE, PHLEGMATIC, ECSTATIC, REALISTIC, STATISTIC, FETTER

Don't disparage
  Marriage.
    True,
It's more phlegmatic
Than ecstatic . . .
More day-to-day
Than hooray . . .
    Too,
It's full of quarrels,
Mixed in morals;
What is more,
It's a bore.
    Yet do
Be realistic:
By statistic,
What fetter
Is better?

Check your preferred definitions below:

| | |
|---|---|
| DISPARAGE | 1. dispute |
| | 2. depress |
| | 3. undervalue |
| | 4. vanish |
| PHLEGMATIC | 1. stubborn |
| | 2. having a stuffy nose |
| | 3. apathetic |
| | 4. defensive |
| ECSTATIC | 1. delicate |
| | 2. saintly |
| | 3. militant |
| | 4. enraptured |
| REALISTIC | 1. serious |
| | 2. conscious |
| | 3. true to life |
| | 4. callous |
| STATISTIC | 1. viewpoint |
| | 2. a numerical datum |
| | 3. heavenly |
| | 4. statist |
| FETTER | 1. a curse |
| | 2. a pancake |
| | 3. a restraint |
| | 4. a necklace |

# 11.

## TYRO, NEURALGIA, NOSTALGIA

You are scarce turned twenty, Algy—a
    Youngster still; at love a tyro.
When you're eighty, with neuralgia,
    You will shiver by the fire, o-
bliged to blow old embers higher; o-
    bliged to poke up old nostalgia.

Check your preferred definitions below:

TYRO
1 despot
2. a chemical
3. a novice
4. acrobat

NEURALGIA
1. senility
2. severe pain radiating along the nerves
3. memories
4. indifference

NOSTALGIA
1. emotion
2. deficiency
3. sentimentality over past occasions; homesickness
4. indecision

# 12.

## RHADAMANTHINE, ANATHEMA

I can prove by Holy Writ
That the Rhadamanthine Pit
Yawns for any man whose riches
Beat the pennies in my breeches.

Heaven's for us poor and meek.
Though I too more pennies seek,
Yet I lay on him who hath 'em a
Bitter Biblical anathema.

Check your preferred definitions below:

RHADAMANTHINE
1. foretelling the future
2. rigorously just
3. Egyptian
4. gigantic

ANATHEMA      1. a proverb
2. a hymn of praise
3. a malediction; a curse
4. authoritative statement

### 13.

## PROGENY, MISOGYNY, MISANTHROPY

For those who wish to dodge any
  Progeny,
I've various advice:
For *him,* misogyny
  May suffice;
For *her,* misanthropy
  Is nice.

But if self-restraint
  Makes you faint,
Or if your shrink says virtue
  May hurt you,
Drugstores have devices
  At low prices.

Check your preferred definitions below:
PROGENY        1. responsibility
2. process
3. miracle
4. offspring, children
MISOGYNY       1. abstinence
2. recklessness
3. disrespect
4. hatred of women
MISANTHROPY    1. pessimism
2. hatred of love
3. obscurity
4. hatred of mankind

### 14.

## APOTHEGM, PRESAGE, OMINOUS, MALIGN, ABATE, IMPENDING, OCULIST

Pray take this apothegm along:
"Beware when nothing's going wrong."
A temporary calm in us

A presage is, and ominous . . .
    Malign.

You claim you see and can abate
Impending hammer blows of fate?
Ah, no; your eyes are blurred indeed.
An oculist is what you need.
    Try mine.

Check your preferred definitions below:

APOTHEGM    1. repartee
   2. atheist
   3. druggist
   4. saying; maxim

PRESAGE    1. tranquilizer
   2. publicity
   3. preventative
   4. augury

OMINOUS    1. overpowering
   2. foreboding evil; menacing
   3. complete
   4. crowded

MALIGN    1. miserly
   2. exhausted
   3. characterized by ill-will; malevolent
   4. whispered

ABATE    1. reduce or lower in force or intensity
   2. depart
   3. entice
   4. disappoint

IMPENDING    1. powerful
   2. about to happen
   3. in custody
   4. incidental

OCULIST    1. a telescope
   2. a prophet
   3. sphinx
   4. a physician who treats diseases of the eye

## 15.

## AGILE, ESCHEW, INCAPACITATED

While still agile, I'll eschew
The traps of lasses such as you.
Once I'm incapacitated,
I'll give up, and we'll be mated.

Check your preferred definitions below:

AGILE
1. aging
2. mischievous
3. capable
4. active

ESCHEW
1. defer
2. reject
3. discuss
4. avoid

INCAPACITATED
1. imprisoned
2. deprived of natural power
3. instructed
4. removed, as a tumor

## 16.

## PRURIENCE, PUBESCENTS, PERVERSION, DOTARD, ADOLESCENT

Let prurience among pubescents
Remain the fringe, and not the essence!
By law laid down of Mede and Persian
Must prurience provoke perversion.
Let honor, modesty, and reason
Foreshorten prurience's season!

(Yet dotards may abandon all their pounds and pence
For one last whiff of adolescent prurience.)

Check your preferred definitions below:

PRURIENCE
1. fastidiousness
2. skin infection
3. caution
4. lascivious desire or thought

PUBESCENTS
1. boils
2. forked lightning
3. adolescents
4. nightmares

PERVERSION
1. snobbery
2. paradox
3. deviance
4. amusement

DOTARD
1. One who dotes
2. Child of low IQ
3. Green-necked duck
4. One whose mind is impaired by age

ADOLESCENT
1. illicit
2. charlatan
3. vital; energetic
4. like a teen-ager

## 17.

### RETROSPECT, FEIGN (a triolet)

I'd say, in retrospect, you
   Only feigned your passion.
I did not reject you;
I'd say in retrospect, you
Found me intellectu-
   ally out of fashion.
I'd say, in retrospect, you
   Only feigned your passion.

Check your preferred definitions below:
RETROSPECT   1. reversal
               2. resumé
               3. admiration
               4. looking back on the past
FEIGN        1. dilute
               2. imagine
               3. prefer
               4. pretend

## 18.

### PHILANDER, UXORIOUS

I once knew a gander
   True to his goose.
He didn't philander,
   Didn't seduce.
Hail, meritorious
   Gander uxorious!

Check your preferred definitions below:
PHILANDER   1. pester
               2. broaden
               3. flirt
               4. fraternize
UXORIOUS    1. elaborate
               2. domineering
               3. considerate
               4. dotingly fond of one's wife

19.

## SEDATELY, DIAPHANOUS, CHERUBIM (a villanelle)

None recalls that I am there,
So sedately do I lie
On the hill in Graveyard Square.

Tranquil is the mouse's lair
In the moss above my thigh;
None recalls that I am there.

Each intent on his affair,
Snake and mole and hare go by
On the hill in Graveyard Square.

Earth, diaphanous as air,
Opens heaven to my eye:
None recalls that I am there.

Cherubim raise wings in prayer,
Unaware of how I spy;
None recalls that I am there
On the hill in Graveyard Square.

Check your preferred definitions below:

SEDATELY
1. unnoticed
2. soberly, calmly
3. matronly
4. rigidly

DIAPHANOUS
1. perfumed
2. breathless
3. light, sunny
4. transparent

CHERUBIM
1. ancient chariots
2. babies
3. musical instruments
4. angels

20.

## POSTHUMOUS

When the time arrives to costume us
In morticians' fin'ry posthumous,

Will we pause before a glass
To see how splendidly we pass?

PREFERRED: PŎS-chŏo-mas

Check your preferred definition below:
POSTHUMOUS  1. old-fashioned
             2. reasonable
             3. after death
             4. temperamental

## 21.

## MYRIAD, BLATANT, PATENT, LATENT, ACUITY, DEFENESTRATE

Your charms, my dear, though myriad,
   Are blatant.
In some prospective period,
   It's patent,
With each of t'other wearièd,
   Some latent
Acuity may make me hate you,
And I may well defenestrate you.

Check your preferred definitions below:

MYRIAD
1. luminous
2. mythical
3. obscure
4. countless

BLATANT
1. whimpering
2. harmful
3. overconfident
4. obtrusive

PATENT
1. relevant
2. certificate
3. obvious
4. glowing

LATENT
1. delayed
2. childish
3. hidden
4. elastic

ACUITY
1. sharpness
2. ambition
3. buffered aspirin
4. hopefulness

DEFENESTRATE
1. intercede
2. expand
3. discard
4. to throw out of a window

## 22.

### AFFLUENCE, OPULENCE

Affluence and opulence
  And I do not agree;
If you are down to thirty cents,
  You're just the same as me.

Check your preferred definitions below:
AFFLUENCE  1. prestige
              2. occult power
              3. tidal wave
              4. wealth
OPULENCE  1. brilliance
              2. riches
              3. potency
              4. celebration

## 23.

### DEMISE

The tears that fell at your demise
  Did ev'ry eyeball drain;
Yet we would pump up new supplies
  If you should rise again.

Check your preferred definition below:
DEMISE  1. arrangement
           2. death
           3. half-measure
           4. short undergarment

## 24.

### INEXPUNGEABLE, FUNGIBLE

One fury alone I have found inexpungeable:
The wrath of a woman who finds herself fungible.

Check your preferred definitions below:

INEXPUNGEABLE  1. permeated by a strong
odor
2. shattered
3. unable to be blotted out
4. inexplicable

FUNGIBLE  1. moldy
2. fragile
3. sarcastic
4. interchangeable

# 25.

## ADDLED, QUIETUS, PICAYUNISH, ADULTEROUS, ASSIGNATION, COGNOSCENTI

The television tube doth treat us
   To lives of addled morals:
Where crack of pistol puts quietus
   To picayunish quarrels;
Where ev'ry innocent flirtation
   Adulterously winds up;
Where we accept an assignation
   Before we make our minds up.

Abortions, madness, thievery,
   That flow from horn of plenty—
In sum, a sav'ry recipe
   To please us cognoscenti.

Check your preferred definitions below:

ADDLED  1. subsequent
2. sizable
3. debatable
4. confused; muddled

QUIETUS  1. vespers
2. death; death blow
3. dimness
4. relaxation

PICAYUNISH  1. petty
2. involving money
3. jealous
4. dark-skinned

ADULTEROUS  1. grown-up, mature
2. seductive
3. thinned with water
4. sexually illicit

| ASSIGNATION | 1. misbehavior |
| | 2. invitation |
| | 3. official signature |
| | 4. appointment for a tryst |
| COGNOSCENTI | 1. Italian aristocrats |
| | 2. wanderers |
| | 3. perfume makers |
| | 4. connoisseurs |

## 26.

### DISHEVELED

A wicked fellow lured a chit—
A maiden, chaste and exquisite—
Into a revel. She said, "Sir,
Be careful not to go too fur—
Though I will not object a whit
If you dishevel me a bit."

Check your preferred definition below:
| DISHEVEL | 1. rumple |
| | 2. serve out |
| | 3. foist upon |
| | 4. uncork |

## 27.

### IMMANENT, IMMINENT, AMOK, AMUCK

Alike in sound are immanent
(Which means "inherent," and is spent
  On philosophic talk),
And imminent (which names a thing
This very instant threatening
  To up and run amok)
(Although amuck will also do;
Amok, amuck—it's up to you.)

Check your preferred definitions below:
| IMMANENT | 1. in the fetal state |
| | 2. subjective, indwelling, intrinsic |
| | 3. difficult to understand |
| | 4. relating to the Stoic school of philosophy |

IMMINENT
1. threatening
2. recent
3. impending
4. in the far future

AMOK
1. manure pile
2. off-color story
3. crazed with murderous frenzy
4. Eskimo funeral ceremony

## 28.

### FLUSTERED

A bustard whose diet was carrion
Was shocked in his views dietarian
   When cooked in a custard
   And served up with mustard.
"I thought," he said, flustered,
"That humans were all vegetarian."

Check your preferred definition below:
FLUSTERED
1. cleaned out
2. relieved
3. upset
4. flickered

## 29.

### CIRCUMSPECT, CLANDESTINE

When I am drinking on the sly
(Lest others should object),
It's clear as gin to me that I
Am being circumspect.
   But she whose bed I nightly rest in
   Asserts my drinking is clandestine.

Check your preferred definitions below:
CIRCUMSPECT
1. indulgent
2. suspicious
3. prudent
4. round-about

CLANDESTINE*
1. tribal rite
2. heir apparent
3. having insight
4. furtive

* See clandestine also in the pronunciation verse on page 172.

## 30.

### ANOMALOUS

When baby's going beddy-bye,
His nightly habit is to cry.
If he drops off without a fuss,
I find the act anomalous,
And spank him till he wakes in pain
To cry himself to sleep again.

Check your preferred definition below:
ANOMALOUS  1. vegetarian
2. abnormal
3. unknown
4. happy-go-lucky

## 31.

### EDIBLE, INCREDIBLE

A giraffe, thinking hay would be edible,
Asked a share from a farmer who fed a bull.
  But he could not, he found,
  Get his head to the ground,
Which the farmer and bull found incredible.

Check your preferred definitions below:
EDIBLE      1. deep-felt
2. qualified
3. astounding
4. eatable
INCREDIBLE  1. written in ink
2. unbelievable
3. not to be eaten
4. effervescent

## 32.

### NAÏVE, NEUROSIS

How naïve
To believe

Halitosis
A neurosis!

Check your preferred definitions below:

NAÏVE
1. inborn
2. ingenuous
3. lighter than air
4. quiet

NEUROSIS
1. nonpartisan
2. hybrid flowers
3. delicacy
4. nervous disorder

## 33.

## LENIENT

A passing lion reassured a bull:
"Don't worry, pal, I'm feeling lenient.
My stomach is already over-full;
To eat you now'd be inconvenient."

Check your preferred definition below:

LENIENT
1. Russian statesman
2. merciful
3. silvery
4. slanting

## LACONIC, EFFICACIOUS, EUPHONIC, LOQUACIOUS

I wooed you in phrases laconic;
'Twas not efficacious.
I shifted to verses euphonic;
You said, "Too loquacious!"

Check your preferred definitions below:

LACONIC
1. concise
2. footman
3. needy
4. fiddling

EFFICACIOUS
1. bubbly
2. disease of horses
3. effective
4. scheming

EUPHONIC   1. pertaining to the telephone
2. pathologically happy
3. related to agreeable sound
4. affected in style
LOQUACIOUS   1. tippling
2. partial
3. exhilarating
4. talkative

## 35.

## TACITURN

Such brooding beauty I discern
   Beside this sea, beneath this sky,
I wish that I could shout and cry—
   But stand here dumb. Too taciturn
      Am I.

Check your preferred definition below:
TACITURN   1. confident
2. bodice
3. driving maneuver
4. untalkative

## 36.

## APATHETIC, ANESTHETIC, DALLIANCE, CARDIACAL, MANIACAL, BUFFOON

Dull was I—as apathetic
As one under anesthetic—
Till your dalliance cardiacal
Put me in a phase maniacal.
Nightly now I play buffoon,
Like the cow that leaped the moon.

Check your preferred definitions below:
APATHETIC   1. pitiable
2. racial policy
3. witty saying
4. listless
ANESTHETIC   1. mood pill
2. bohemian dance
3. aesthetically displeasing
4. an agent causing unconsciousness to pain

| DALLIANCE | 1. style of a surrealist painter |
| | 2. dawdling; amorous play |
| | 3. nickname of the Dallas Chamber of Commerce |
| | 4. neurotic fear of movement |
| CARDIACAL | 1. pertaining to the College of Cardinals |
| | 2. characteristic flight of the cardinal bird |
| | 3. pertaining to the heart or, figuratively, love |
| | 4. devoted to bridge, rummy, hearts, etc. |
| MANIACAL | 1. manly |
| | 2. manacled, fettered |
| | 3. relating to the origin of man |
| | 4. mad |
| BUFFOON | 1. one who bluffs |
| | 2. a clownish jester |
| | 3. a scapegoat |
| | 4. a destructive oriental windstorm |

## 37.

## CONGENITAL, CHLORINE

Though men breathe oxygen, it all
Is happenstance congenital.
They say in constellations foreign
They customarily breathe chlorin'.

Check your preferred definitions below:

| CONGENITAL | 1. inborn |
| | 2. agreeable |
| | 3. marital |
| | 4. bisexual |
| CHLORINE | 1. chorus girl |
| | 2. ritual |
| | 3. bragging |
| | 4. bleaching agent |

## 38.

### GLIBLY, MAGNANIMOUS, FLAUNT, FLOUT, ANIMUS

Good pal, how glibly you proceed,
With rhetoric magnanimous
To flaunt your care for those in need!
If word less clearly flouted deed
'Twould be more difficult to read
Behind your words, your animus.

Check your preferred definitions below:

GLIBLY
1. with careful calculation
2. eloquently
3. foolishly
4. fluently but superficially

MAGNANIMOUS
1. majestic
2. clamorous
3. generously noble
4. extremely complicated

FLAUNT
1. bombard
2. show off
3. emphasize
4. mock, sneer

FLOUT
1. challenge
2. explain
3. scorn
4. flutter

ANIMUS
1. bitter hostility
2. effervescence
3. automaton
4. solemnity

## 39.

### PERSPICACITY, PUGNACITY (a lai)

I lack perspicacity
To know my capacity
    For wine.
Wine stirs my pugnacity;
Better a glass o' tea
    For mine.

Check your preferred definitions below:

PERSPICACITY
1. deduction
2. sarcasm
3. temerity
4. discernment

PUGNACITY
1. altruism
2. belligerency
3. depravity
4. amorousness

## 40.

## BAFFLEMENT, GREGARIOUS

What bafflement is mine and yours
That buses always come in fours!
Perhaps they are gregarious;
Or maybe they're afraid of us.

Check your preferred definitions below:

BAFFLEMENT
1. trickery
2. shame
3. puzzlement
4. barricade

GREGARIOUS
1. dangerous
2. clerical
3. beguiling
4. sociable

## 41.

## GAUDY, DEBONAIR, CAJOLED, PANOPLY, ATTRIBUTE, CACOPHONY

A Parrot (gaudy, debonair),
    Who met a Raven in a tree,
Cajoled her thus: "My love I swear:
    Come, fly away and marry me."
Quoth Raven: "Nay: the black I wear
    Would shame your flashy panoply.
Name just one attribute we share!"
    Said pretty Poll: "Cacophony."
"Of caws, of caws," the Raven said,
    And noisily the two were wed.

Check your preferred definitions below:

GAUDY
1. boisterous
2. speckled
3. garishly colored
4. proud

DEBONAIR
1. youthful
2. light and feathery
3. musical
4. jaunty or suave

CAJOLED
1. coaxed
2. tempted
3. guided
4. flirted

PANOPLY
1. broad view
2. magnificent covering
3. Greek arena game
4. awning

ATTRIBUTE
1. temperament
2. characteristic
3. allocation
4. pattern

CACOPHONY
1. animal cries
2. ability to fly
3. jarring sound
4. oratory

## 42.

## ENERVATED, REGENERATED

Gen, when I'm in the dumps,
  Exhausted, enervated—
You smile, and my heart jumps—
  By Gen regenerated.

Check your preferred definitions below:

ENERVATED
1. irritated
2. neurologically damaged
3. deprived of strength
4. depressed

REGENERATED
1. augmented
2. renewed
3. prescribed
4. stabilized

# 43.

## ANACHRONISTIC, OBSOLETE, SCRUPULOUSLY

I told a dragon, "You're anachronistic;
   You're obsolete; indeed, you are extinct."
Though I was scrupulously realistic,
   He gulped me down. I understand he winked.

Check your preferred definitions below:

ANACHRONISTIC    1. revolutionary
                           2. puzzling
                           3. out of its proper time
                           4. disguised

OBSOLETE    1. old-fashioned
                           2. many-sided
                           3. no longer in use
                           4. console of a piano

SCRUPULOUSLY    1. uncertainly
                           2. punctiliously
                           3. mistakenly
                           4. pushily

# 44.

## ICONOCLAST, SYCOPHANTIC

Of that iconoclast beware
   Who comes to pay a call,
And rips your paintings from the wall,
   And wrecks your Wedgwood ware.

"Desist!" you cry in manner frantic;
   "Treat not my treasures so!"
"I only smash them, sir, to show
   That I'm not sycophantic."

Check your preferred definitions below:

ICONOCLAST    1. schemer
                           2. Greek Orthodox priest
                           3. attacker of traditional ideas
                           4. vandal

SYCOPHANTIC    1. identical
                           2. flattering
                           3. overreactive
                           4. tractable

## 45.

### PROPHYLACTIC, PANACEA

Love's my sickness; offer me a
Prophylactic—panacea.
(I'll extend my thanks to you,
Holding nose, and dumping brew.)

Check your preferred definitions below:

PROPHYLACTIC  1. logical argument
2. an antidote
3. protection
4. bacteria

PANACEA  1. wide-angle view
2. a cure-all
3. Turkish harem
4. barrier

## 46.

### PALLID, LIVID, LURID, FERVID, LUCID, MORBID, CANDID, SORDID

When the moon is thin and pallid,
I stay home and eat a salad.
When the moon emerges vivid,
My reflected face turns livid.
When the waxing moon grows lurid,
Odd compulsions sweep my poor id.
When the moon swells plump and curvèd,
Then my passions grow more fervid;
When it's gibbous, I'll be deucèd
If it's right to call me lucid.
When the moon is fully orbèd,
I am lunatic; I'm morbid.
Under full moon, to be candid,
I do things that ne'er good man did:
Do things no one e'er before did:
Some things heavenly, some sordid.

Check your preferred definitions below:

PALLID  1. narrow
2. doleful
3. wan
4. marginal

| LIVID | 1. intense |
| | 2. flashy |
| | 3. bilious |
| | 4. having discolored skin |
| LURID | 1. golden |
| | 2. glowing through a haze |
| | 3. extravagant |
| | 4. seductive |
| FERVID | 1. obstinate |
| | 2. impassioned |
| | 3. emaciated |
| | 4. drunk |
| LUCID | 1. easily understood |
| | 2. bashful |
| | 3. friendly |
| | 4. amorous |
| MORBID | 1. obsolete |
| | 2. unscrupulous |
| | 3. emotional |
| | 4. preoccupied with gloomy matters |
| CANDID | 1. moonstruck |
| | 2. without reserve |
| | 3. tactless |
| | 4. vacuous |
| SORDID | 1. earthy |
| | 2. guilty |
| | 3. vile |
| | 4. variegated |

# 47.

## DROVES, PROFANE, WANTON, THEORETICAL

The laddies in droves upon Betty call,
With aims more profane than poetical.
  She welcomes as flattering
  Their wanton young chattering,
But insists that it stay theoretical.

Check your preferred definitions below:

| DROVES | 1. mass of people |
| | 2. jitney buses |
| | 3. pigeons |
| | 4. pathways |
| PROFANE | 1. learned |
| | 2. lyrical |
| | 3. vulgar |
| | 4. gaseous |
| WANTON | 1. stingy |
| | 2. pleading |
| | 3. lewd |
| | 4. careless |

THEORETICAL   1. imprecise
              2. speculative
              3. religious
              4. algebraic

## 48.

## CANDOR, NEFARIOUS, SEMANTIC, SLANDER, DANDER

Let me speak with candor.
Contracts saying and/or
Hide within them various
Legal tricks nefarious,
Legal tricks semantic,
Booby-traps for slander.
Brave your lawyer's dander:
Ban this legal antic.

Check your preferred definitions below:
CANDOR    1. frankness
          2. humility
          3. constancy
          4. neighbor
NEFARIOUS 1. gloomy
          2. basic
          3. evil
          4. intricate
SEMANTIC  1. incomplete
          2. prejudiced
          3. warned by signaling
          4. referring to meaning in language
SLANDER   1. lizard
          2. defamation of character
          3. massacre
          4. landslide
DANDER    1. cavern
          2. temper
          3. wattles
          4. ostentation

# 49.

## EGREGIOUS, SACRILEGIOUS

A choir boy, when hymns became tedious,
Kissed a choir girl—a sin most egregious.
  Though the preacher's her pop,
  She whispered, "Don't stop;
It's such fun to be sacrilegious!"

Check your preferred definitions below:

EGREGIOUS
1. sociable
2. foreign
3. outrageous
4. comical

SACRILEGIOUS
1. martyred
2. holy
3. backbreaking
4. impious

# 50.

## INDEFATIGABLE, SUPERSEDE, SIMULATE

When I for overdue promotion buck,
Some eager, indefatigable schmuck
(First to unlock the office, last to lock,
Who never raises eye to laggard clock)
Will always supersede me—this although
I'm first man out when it is time to go,
And simulate hard labor when the boss
Speaks in a tone that's noticeably cross.
It goes to show that brains have lost their worth:
The stupid are inheriting the earth.

PREFERRED: in-dĭ-FĀT-ə-ga-bəl

Check your preferred definitions below:

INDEFATIGABLE
1. overworked
2. tireless
3. defenseless
4. energetic

| SUPERSEDE | 1. scorn |
|---|---|
| | 2. ascend |
| | 3. replace or succeed |
| | 4. overproduce |
| SIMULATE | 1. anticipate |
| | 2. simplify |
| | 3. substitute |
| | 4. pretend |

# 51.

## MALEVOLENT, PROPAGATED, DEGENERATED, PREVALENT, BENEVOLENT

Malevolent,
Enraged at heaven's curses,
    The devil lent
To Eve two pretty verses.
    Like hamsters they
Their species propagated,
    While day by day
The breed degenerated.
    Too prevalent
Is rhyme, and growing worse;
O Lord benevolent,
    Blot out this verse.

Check your preferred definition below:

| MALEVOLENT | 1. turbulent |
|---|---|
| | 2. malicious |
| | 3. ingenious |
| | 4. hostile |
| PROPAGATED | 1. advanced |
| | 2. classified |
| | 3. bred |
| | 4. increased |
| DEGENERATED | 1. deviated |
| | 2. survived |
| | 3. exterminated |
| | 4. deteriorated |
| PREVALENT | 1. noxious |
| | 2. widespread |
| | 3. explicit |
| | 4. extravagant |
| BENEVOLENT | 1. fair-minded |
| | 2. joyful |
| | 3. kindly |
| | 4. perceptive |

## 52.

### INTREPID, AUDACIOUS

A mouse that hounds a cat about
Intrepid is, without a doubt—
Audacious, too, I understand.
And yet, upon the other hand,
What life insurance company
Would issue it a policy?

Check your preferred definitions below:

INTREPID   1. trespassing
2. curious
3. courageous
4. alarmed

AUDACIOUS   1. acutely aware
2. swift
3. audible
4. daring

## 53.

### AWRY

The cat, who was flustered
When caught in the custard,
Went still more awry
By bolting the pie.

Check your preferred definition below:

AWRY†   1. feverish
2. amiss or askew
3. rampant
4. guilty

## 54.

### INSINUATE, SINEW

(There is an oddity about this verse: it has no rhyme. Each line
has the same end-sound.)

† See awry also on page 206.

I have heard your friends insinu-
ate some naughty imp that's in you
Leads you on from sin to sin; you
Sin in bone and blood and sinew—
Sin in bone and blood and sinew
From some naughty imp that's in you.

Check your preferred definitions below:
INSINUATE   1. secure
            2. hint at
            3. fabricate
            4. interpret
SINEW   1. appearance
            2. insight
            3. contest
            4. tendon

## 55.

## MEDIATOR

(I found the following verse in some old correspondence. I have
not the faintest recollection of writing it, but assume I must have.
If, however, *you* wrote it, send me an indignant letter and I will
print a groveling apology in the next edition of this book. Assuming, of course, that there is a next edition of this book.)

Medora, the lioness down at the zoo,
Fell out with her keeper, Ms. Sydney LaRue.
Medy scorned all resort to a fact-finding board—
Outside interference that feline abhorred.
"God backed up the right," said the lioness later;
"Who battles for justice needs no mediator."
    (Medy ate 'er.)

Check your preferred definition below:
MEDIATOR   1. interceptor
            2. wanderer
            3. intermediary
            4. philosopher

## 56.

## PARADOX, DILEMMA

When Jack was twenty-one or such,
  And Jill scarce woman bloomed,
So hot each blazed at t'other's touch,
  They should have been consumed.

*From tree to tree fire leaps its way:*
*Yet faithful they, yet faithful they.*

When Jack had dimmed to fifty-five,
  And Jill was long unkissed,
They puffed old coals to keep them live,
  And hunted heavens missed.

*When ash of love had died away,*
*Unfaithful they, unfaithful they.*

### Moral

Sure, virtue's easy for an ox;
And yet I pose a paradox:
Why blood when hot obeys love's rules,
But grows unfaithful as it cools.
*Dilemma's the expiring fire*
*That trades commitment for desire.*

Check your preferred definitions below:
PARADOX   1. a situation beyond belief
          2. something seemingly opposed to
             common sense that may yet be
             true
          3. a counter-argument
          4. first phase of a solar eclipse
DILEMMA   1. an impasse
          2. temptation
          3. an impossible dream
          4. a quandary

# ELEVEN

## USAGE

*Canute:*

When King Canute ordered the sea to stop rising, it rose anyway. The sea of language is as inexorable. I have friends who turn purple when confronted with a split infinitive or a preposition at the end of a sentence—just as I turn purple when I see a beautiful woman chewing gum. But infinitives are still split, prepositions still end sentences, and otherwise beautiful women still chew their cuds. Yesterday's sacred cow may be tomorrow's scapegoat. I do not ask that you abide by every current rule of usage; they are changing under your eyes. But I do ask that to the best of your ability you learn the current rules, so that if you break them you will know what you are doing. It was once said that a gentleman is one who never hurts another's feelings unintentionally; surely a civilized speaker is one who does not break the accepted canons unaware. Suppose you consider some grammatical convention ridiculous and outdated, but lack the courage to discard it. In that event, I suggest you seek out moral support from someone, or something, that at the critical moment will whisper into your ear, "Don't let that infinitive walk all over you, man—*split* it!" No matter if our helper, like the two below, exists only inside your mind:

## TWO LITTLE HELPERS

I have two little helpers whom I love as kin and kith.
The first is at my beck and call to end a sentence with.
The second is a woodsman with an ax by which he lives:
He uses it to violently split infinitives.

*Rules Frequently Ignored:*

Quixotic grammarians spend their lifetimes breaking lances against the thick scales of grammatical dragons. These dragons are born unnoticed in the verbal wilderness, but finally grow so big that they venture into the open. They spend their lives bellowing and breathing flame, and either die for lack of maidens to feed on or live on forever. They do not really devour maidens; hay suits them better; they are quite harmless, really. They are also quite invulnerable. They do not appear to notice, much less resent, the rattle of spears against their plating.

Though hundreds and even thousands of these dragons roam our streets, the heroes who attack them tend to concentrate on a trifling few, and the thickest-scaled at that. Here are some that have ignored our attacks:

·*Infer* for *Imply.* You infer a meaning from what I imply. Simple, right? But the mob insists on using the two words interchangeably. (If you fall victim to this error, take comfort from history. Two hundred years ago, imply and infer *did* have the same meaning. And in those days, by the way, the possessive pronoun *its* was properly spelled *it's,* a spelling that today proclaims an illiterate. As I say, times change. Still, I feel strongly the distinction between imply and infer):

## IMPLY, INFER

What I imply, I hint. What you infer
Is what you think I hinted. Better, sir,
To say "hello" in error for "good-by"
Than say "infer" in error for "imply."

·*Media* as a singular noun. Medium is the singular; media is plural, representing collectively such disposable tissue as newspapers, pamphlets, magazines, and books like this one, not to mention television and radio. You, the public, in your wisdom, have made a singular word plural. It is your right—just as it is my right to respond by weeping into the Hermit Hoar's beer.

·*Criteria* is another plural that has become hopelessly singular, and so singularly hopeless:

## CRITERIA

There's but one
Criterion.
Folks inferia
Say "one criteria."

· *Flaunt* for *Flout*. Flaunt shows off; flout mocks or insults.

## FLAUNT, FLOUT

I preen myself on my mustache;
That is to say, I flaunt it.
   Unhappily,
   My *chères amies*
Insist that they don't want it,
And I should do without it.
   I flaunt it.
   They flout it.

· *Lady* for *Woman*. Cultural chauvinism appears to dictate that any term for a woman (and often for a man) shall degenerate. Latin *carus*, "beloved," gradually turned into whore; housewife into hussy. A lady, once a woman of superior rank, is now any woman (as in 'ladies' room'; 'gents' is a male equivalent) and is sometimes something worse ('lady of the night').

*Exit Rigidity:*
Bearing in mind Spenser's dictum, "Be bold, be bold . . . be not too bold," check the usages below that you consider acceptable in informal conversation. Then we will compare your opinion with that of a panel of language experts:

### OCTET OF OUGHT AND OUGHTN'T

|  | Yes | No |
|---|---|---|
| Your eyes are different *than* mine. | — | — |
| *Due* to the cost, I don't drink wine. | — | — |
| His interference makes me *mad*. | — | — |
| He acts as if he *was* my dad. | — | — |
| *The reason* I am blue is not | — | — |
| *Because* of you. What has he *got*? | — | — |
| We had a *nice* time buying clothes. | — | — |
| Let's walk a little *further*, Rose. | — | — |

Strictly speaking—at least in formal writing—you should shun most of the above locutions, for these reasons:

·Different *than*. Than is a conjunction, not a preposition. When referring to an object, say "different from."

·*Due* to the cost. When writing, use instead the prepositional "because of." Due is a predicate adjective (the bill is *due*), not a preposition.

·Makes me *mad*. True, *mad* once meant "deranged," not "enraged." But common usage has made it synonymous with "furious," even on paper. Unless you are writing a doctor's essay.

·As if he *was* my dad. A condition contrary to fact requires the subjunctive. Write (and say) "He acts as if he were my dad."

·*The reason is because*. Because added to reason creates a redundancy. Write "the reason is that."

·What has he *got?* Got is an imprecise verb. Write "What does he have?"

·We had a *nice* time. It is more exact to say "we had a pleasant time," reserving nice for "precise, subtle." But the latter sense is dying out.

·*Further*. Further refers to degree, farther to distance. Write "farther."

Here is how the panelists of the *Harper Dictionary of Contemporary Usage,* of whom I was one, feel about the above words in conversation:

·Different *than*. Accepted when the object of the preposition is a clause: "Please inform us if your address is different *than* it was." I agree.

·*Due* to. Accepted. I agree.

·*Mad* for *angry*. Accepted. I agree.

·As if he *was* (contrary to fact). Accepted resignedly. I disagree.

·What has he *got?* The panel ignored this. Even in conversation, got, though inevitable, reflects lazy thinking. (But I use it regularly.)

·*The reason is because*. Best avoided, says the panel, as being "somewhat redundant." I agree, omitting the "somewhat."

·*Nice* for *pleasant*. Overworked, but accepted. "Only in a few instances does it retain its original meaning of 'exact or precise,' as in 'a nice distinction.'" I agree.

·*Further*. Eighty per cent of the panelists distinguish between farther (measuring physical distance) and further (representing degree or quantity). I agree.

Where a violation of accepted usage clearly makes a better sentence, go ahead; stiffness and woodenness are worse than an occasional error. Do not be so conservative that you feel unnatural. On the other hand, correct speech, though it may seem unnatural at first, could eventually become a bosom buddy. Give it a chance.

(When caught in a grammatical slip, as is bound to happen, take comfort; even the Preamble to the Constitution of the United States contains a blooper:

"We the People of the United States," it begins, "in Order to form a more perfect Union . . ." Well, perfect is perfect. Nothing could be more perfect than that. The Founding Fathers meant to write, "More nearly perfect." But two hundred years have sanctioned their error, and I expect that we will all go right on saying "more perfect." Unless, of course, we correct the Preamble by constitutional amendment.)

Ernest Tucker posted in the Toronto *Sun* the following baker's dozen of rules regarding grammar:

1. Don't use no double negatives.
2. Make each pronoun agree with their antecedents.
3. Join clauses good, like a conjunction should.
4. About them sentence fragments.
5. When dangling, watch your participles.
6. Verbs has got to agree with their subjects.
7. Just between you and I, case is important too.
8. Don't write run-on sentences they are hard to read.
9. Don't use commas, which aren't important.
10. Try to not ever split infinitives.
11. It is important to use apostrophe's correctly.
12. Proofread your writing to see if you any words out.
13. Corect speling is essential.

*Another Thought:*

## ALTHOUGH INFORMAL SPEECH IS FREE
(a thirteen-line rondel)

Although informal speech is free,
   It isn't quite as free as air.
You *must* not say: "This here"; "That there";
   "I don't need nothing"; "Maybe me

And him can come"; "When we was three";
   "He don't."—You *must*n't! Don't you dare!—
Although informal speech is free,
   It isn't quite as free as air.

"Now you have did it!" must not be,
   And "irregardless" gets the air.
   "He done"; "I seen"—another pair

To sweep away with the debris,
Although informal speech is free.

*Logic in Grammar:*

"There was a wealthy old man in London," said the Hermit
Hoar, "who brought his lawyer a holographic will that began, 'I,
John So-and-so, of Such-and-such a parish, being of sound mind
and body, God be thanked,' and ended, 'The remainder of my estate I leave to my deceased wife.'"

"Doubtless a slip of the pen. He must have meant my 'beloved'
wife."

"No, no. The fact is, he had never married."

"Then he was crazy."

"Not by his lights. By his lights he was logical. As a man of
property, distinction, and fullness of years, he considered it reasonable that he should have married. He therefore assumed that he
had married. But he knew he had no wife; hence, she must have
died. Grammarians are constantly falling into that sort of trap."

"Uncle Allie," I said, "once wrote:

## WHY NOT?

The verse you write
   You say is written
All rules despite,
   But not despitten
The gas you light
   Is never litten.

The things you drank
   Were doubtless drunk
The boy you spank
   Is never spunk;
The friend you thank
   Is never thunk.

Suppose you speak,
   Then you have spoken,
But if you sneak
   You have not snoken.
The shoes that squeak
   Have never squoken.

A dog will bite,
   Likewise has bitten,
With all his might,
   But not his mitten.

You fly your kite,
But not your kitten."

— Anonymous

"Sometimes," said the Hermit Hoar, "you grow too permissive.
English is frequently illogical; but there could be no English without logic."

"Of course," I said. "Moderation, I say, in all things—even the
logic of tenses. Now, what does tense indicate?"

"When an action occurs, has occurred, may have occurred, or
will occur. Except when it means uptight."

"Exactly. It means uptight in the title of the verse I am about to
read to you. But the tenses referred to in the verse itself are of the
other sort."

"Do you mind if I draw another beer before you start?" asked
the Hermit Hoar, rather wistfully, I thought.

"You can listen while you turn the spindle:"

## A TENSE SITUATION

*The condign punishment of Professor Jones, a logical grammarian*

Best plump for inconsistency
In diction pedagogical;
You'll rue it if you're overly
Grammatically logical.

A logical professor chap
Of intellect immense,
Named Jones, resolved to bridge the gap
That sunders Tense from Sense:

"I'll tell no more in classroom tiffs
How 'was' from 'will be' differs—
Why, if Conditionals are Ifs,
Subjunctives must be Iffers,"

Our Jones exclaimed. "Nought's new to thought
That's underneath the sun:
The Present and the Future ought
To be construed as one."

Then as he spoke, his form grew dim,
More cumulus than clay;
The final words we heard from him
Seemed very far away:

"I did, I do, I will maintain
The First contains the Last

In endless metalogic chain:
Whatever Is, is Past."

And on that fainting, final word,
Jones vanished as in dreams;
Which shows that logic is absurd
    When carried to extremes.


The Hermit Hoar brought the foaming mugs.
"Here's one more verse," I said—"on comparatives:"

## COMPARATIVES

If comparatives you double,
You are in semantic trouble.
Out of thousands, I name four:
    More better,
    More wetter.
    More brighter,
    More lighter.
        Pray omit the "more."

Yet I must allow that it
Does not bother me a bit
When you tell me after dinner
I'm more fatter than more thinner.
    That's what dinner's for.


*Syntax:*

The Hermit Hoar said, "Do you really think such verses will help
your readers to talk better?"

"At least," I said, "they won't talk worse, and one has to run
hard in this world to stay in the same place. As a matter of fact, I
am also going to deliver a brief lecture on syntax."

"Syntax," said the Hermit Hoar. "Sentence structure. I thought
you had been discussing that all along."

"How does love, that anneals man and maid, differ from syntax,
that joins word and word, sentence and sentence?"

"In just about every way I can think of," said the Hermit Hoar.

"I am building up to a little joke. A pun, if you will, contained in
a verse."

"I suspected something of the sort."

I read gently:

## ON THE FUTILITY OF TRYING TO MAKE
## ENDS MEET

A lady with a laughing eye,
Who charged for going beddy-bye
A most inordinate amount,
Still overdrew her bank account.
The highest fees for sin she set—
Yet found her Syntax higher yet.

For a moment there was silence in the solemn cell. Then the Hermit Hoar said, rather more quietly than was usual for him, "My lad, how near are you to the end of the book?"

"I am not quite sure. I thought of touching on several more points. Syllepsis, for instance."

"Define syllepsis for me, lad."

"It is a word that governs two or more words in a sentence, but formally applies to only one of them. It confuses me, though."

## SYL-LEP-SIS

SYL- is for Silly;
LEP- is for Leapt;
SIS is for Sister.
These I accept.
As for what SYL-LEP-SIS means,
I don't know beans.

I had never seen the Hermit Hoar unsure of himself; but his face seemed a little troubled as I continued. "I'll read some examples from Dickens:"

There was a great fizzing and banging of guns, and starting of ladies—and then a mine was sprung, to the gratification of everybody—and when the mine had gone off, the military and the company followed its example, and went off too.

"Very well, gentlemen," said Mr. Pickwick, rising in person and wrath at the same time; "you shall hear from my solicitor, gentlemen."

All the girls were in tears and white muslin.

Miss Bolo rose from the table considerably agitated, and went straight home, in a flood of tears, and a sedan-chair.

He knew not on whom to vent his grief and wrath, until fortunately bethinking himself of the Lord Chamberlain who had

brought him home, he struck off his pension and his head together.

> . . . and to dinner they went with good digestion waiting on
> appetite, and health on both, and a waiter on all three.*

The Hermit Hoar still seemed troubled. "Enjoyable indeed," he
said, "but are you sure that syllepsis, entertaining as it may be—or
your version of syntax, for that matter—will help anyone to speak
better English?"

"A little extra background will do no harm," I said firmly.
"Word origins, for instance. I have said from the start that the more
you know about a word the better you and the word will get along."

"But there is a limit—" said the Hermit Hoar.

"Word origins," I repeated. "Etymology. My preferred authority
on etymology is Thomas Jefferson Allen, stepson of Josiah Allen's
wife."

"He is not on my list of authorities."

"Then you have never read *Samantha at the Centennial*, by
Josiah Allen's wife.† Here is Thomas J.'s explanation to his step-
mother as to why a debating school should be called a lyceum. You
will agree that it is an etymological masterpiece."

"Mmm."

I read:

> "Says Thomas J. to me, says he, 'I hain't a word to say ag'inst
> your callin' it Debatin'-school, only I know you are so kinder
> scientific and philosophical, that I hate to see you usin' a word
> that haint got science to back it up. Now this word Lyceum,'
> says he, 'is derived from the dead languages, and from them
> that is most dead. It is from the Greek and the Injun; a kind
> of half-breed. Ly, is from the Greek, and signifies and means a
> big story, or, in other words, a falsehood; and ce-um is from
> the Injun; and it all means, "see 'em lie." ' "

"Willard," said the Hermit Hoar, "you are no longer writing a
textbook."

"Of course I am."

"No—you have reached the point where you are merely amusing
yourself. I do not mean to put down your book, lad. You have
given some good advice. Anyone who follows it faithfully will
speak more acceptable and enjoyable English, no doubt about it.
But if you have not managed to improve a reader's speaking habits
by now, you are not likely to."

* These excerpts from *The Pickwick Papers* were called to my attention by
Bob Knille.

† Josiah Allen's Wife" was a pseudonym of Marietta Holley (1836–1926).

His voice was measured and serious; even Author Unknown looked at him inquiringly.

"What are you telling me, Hermit Hoar?"

"I am saying that the time has come to quit."

The idea had not even occurred to me. It took a moment to sink in. Then I saw the Hermit Hoar smiling at me. Slowly I smiled back.

"You know," I said, "I hadn't put it into words, but I was getting pretty tired of that book. Why should I go on turning sows' purses into silk ears?"

"The point could not be better phrased," said the Hermit Hoar, handing me a freshly opened bottle of beer. "You have only one message, after all."

We lofted our bottles and cried in chorus:

"Say it my way!"

# AFTERWORD

I am an abstemious man. Within reason, of course; I do not go so far as to insist, say, that lips that touch liquor shall never touch mine.

Still, when I have finally completed a manuscript, I consider a modest celebration permissible, even mandatory. So after typing the last word of SAY IT MY WAY, I tramped in jig time, Author Unknown stalking beside me, to the solemn cell of the Hermit Hoar. The three of us (for Author Unknown is no slouch about lapping beer) plunged directly into drinking, singing, and howling. Outside, the twilight darkened, the moon rose, and a band of crows circled, excitedly cawing. Their presence annoyed Author Unknown; he stalked back and forth between the two grimy windows, standing with his front paws on first one sill and then the other, warning off the crows with deep, peremptory barks. They ignored him.

As once before, the Hermit Hoar and I toasted all the languages we could recall, including one I had just come across named QWERTYUIOP.* We sang hymns, ballads, and lewd songs. We heaped alder logs on the fire; but the fire was not drawing well, the wind being from the east; it pushed in through chinks, causing

---

* Typewriter language, created by Ilene Astrahan and Alex Gross.

smoke to eddy about the room. When the puffs reached the empty rocker it would nod courteously.

I had been working hard, and after several hours my energy flagged. I nodded, pinched myself, nodded again . . . When I clawed my way out of sleep, the barking of Author Unknown and the screaming of the crows had mounted to an ear-splitting cacophony.

My eyes, blurrily taking in the empty rocking chair, suddenly blurred no longer. For the chair was not empty at all. It was filled to overflowing with such a figure of a man as, once seen, can never be erased from the mind. He was huge, fat, and ancient—a man with a dewlap like a bull's, a belly like a beer barrel, and a face like a withered gourd standing on its stem end. His sweater was of the knitted Irish variety, and thick-lensed glasses magnified his eyes.

"Uncle Allie!" I cried. "But you have been dead these four years!"

"And shall be four million more, I shouldn't wonder," his high, familiar voice replied. "Come hug your old uncle, my boy." This I did with tears and right good will; his flesh was warm and solid in my arms.

"First, a beer all around," said Uncle Allie. . . . "Ah! that's better; one does grow dry. And now, my boy, I have a message for you."

I must have looked as confused as I felt.

"The Anonymous clan feels you are in the wrong way," said Mr. Anonymous gravely.

"What have I done?" I asked, concerned; for reproach from Uncle Allie at such a reunion as this was the last thing I had expected.

"Little, my boy. Too little. Even that little, you have signed with your own name. And if I may be permitted an advisory, trivial stuff it is." (Author Unknown had ceased his barking. He was now seated by the rocker, having managed to arrange his head so that it rested in Uncle Allie's lap. Uncle Allie was scratching the dog behind the ears.)

"Dear Uncle Allie," I said, "I am sorry—so sorry!" And I meant it. I loved him.

He took a copious swig of his beer, and removed his hand from Author Unknown long enough to press mine. "Not to worry, my boy," he said. "The Hermit Hoar" (who sat drinking placidly alongside us, apparently disregarding the entire conversation) "has taught you the first half of 'what is bliss, and which the way'—"

At this the Hermit Hoar shook himself and raised a forefinger. "Come, my lad, and drink some beer!" the three of us shouted in chorus.

"But you still have not been instructed in the second half. Your

Anonymous kinfolk, not to mention my old friends Trad, Idem, and Ibid, want you to learn the whole secret while there is still time."

"Dear uncle, I am all ears."

"It is simple, really," he said, letting the last of the beer run down his throat and wiping his mouth with the back of his hand. "Simply bear in mind . . ."

He pushed against the arms of the chair to rise and face me. The Hermit Hoar lined up beside him, standing stiff and straight. Without surprise I noted a third figure; Author Unknown was standing there too, tall and upright as a man.

". . . that you should never say it your way, but . . ."

His voice was fading; all three figures appeared to be merging with the smoke. As I strained for a last sight of them, three voices, including, I swear, that of Author Unknown, floated back across the gap growing between us:

"Say . . . it . . . *ou-u-ur* . . . way!"

I woke at home, in the cottage that had once belonged to Mr. Anonymous. He was gone; so was the Hermit Hoar; so was Author Unknown. I have seen none of them since.

Nor have I drunk a beer.

# VERSES TO IMPROVE
# YOUR PRONUNCIATION

# THE SCHWA

Dictionaries use diacritical markings to distinguish different pronunciations of the same letter of the alphabet. Thus, ā is pronounced as in bay; â as in care (the difference, though fine, is real); ă is in add; ä as in arm. There is no way to communicate the exact pronunciation of a word in writing except through these diacritical markings. I use as few as possible in listing preferred pronunciations in this book. One diacritical marking, however, is used here repeatedly. That is the *schwa*. The schwa (ə), indicating an unaccented, neutral vowel, is indispensable because all vowels, if pronounced with minimum stress, are identical in sound. The schwa represents that shared sound, the next thing to no sound at all.

Some time ago, I wrote:

> The ə on his diurnəl rounds
> Is minəs all but minər sounds;
> Yet may, phonetəcəsts əgree,
> Unite a wide vəriəty
> Of audəble phənomənə:
> Aə, Eə, Iə, Oə . . .
> Uə.

Apart from the usual pronunciation symbols for long or short vowels, these also appear in the following pages:

> ä=as in *cart* or *cot*
> ô=as in *all* or *law*
> ü=as in *few*

## ACCEPT, ACCEDE, ACCESSORY, SUCCINCT

In words with double C's, express
C first as K, and then as S:
A*k*-SEPT, a*k*-SEDE, a*k*-SESS-ory.
(One time there was a silly lout
Who always left the K sound out.
He said a*ss*-EPT, he said su*ss*-INCT;
He luckily became extinct
Before he could propose that we
Reverse the sounds of double C
And say a*ss*-KEPT, a*ss*-KESS-ory.)

Check your preferred definition below:
SUCCINCT  1. produced by sucking
2. brief or hasty; curt
3. treacherous and engulfing, as quicksand
4. subject to fainting spells

## ATHLETE

An ATH-leet and an ATH-e-leet are in my
    class at school.
The ATH-lete is a scholar, while the
    ATH-e-leet's a fool.

PREFERRED:  ĀTH-lete

## ATTACKED

A cub said, "My rump was just smackted
By a wicked old man I'd attackted.
    Although I'm a bear, he
    Did not find me scary;
Dear Mommy, what was it I lackted?"

The mother bear said, "Lad,
Your English drove him mad.
    He reacted
    To 'attackted.'
    If you'd said
    'Attacked,' instead,
That old man would have fled."

PREFERRED:  ə-TĂKT

## AVIATOR, RADIATOR, RADIO

Jack says AV-vi-a-tor
For AY-vi-a-tor.
Jill says RAD-di-ay-tor
For RAY-di-ay-tor.
Which mistake is greater?
I don't know.
    Oh—

Al Smith* said "RAD-di-o."
*That* was a baddy-o.

> PREFERRED: Ā-vē-āt-ər
> RĀ-dē-ā-tər
> RĀ-dē-ō
> (Nobody makes these mistakes any more; I just wanted an excuse for slipping in "baddy-o.")

## BICYCLE, MOTORCYCLE

Michael's bicycle
Rhymes with icicle.
His motorcycle
Rhymes with Michael.

> PREFERRED: BĪ-sĭk-əl
> MŌT-ər-SĪ-kəl

## BIOPSY, AUTOPSY

When Cottontail's heartsy went stopsy,
The coroner's verdict was dropsy.
Peter, though, grumbled to Mopsy,
"I know he was turvy and topsy,
Flipsy and flapsy and flopsy,
Hipsy and hepsy and hopsy;
But when did he have a bye-OP-sy?
I think I'll demand an au-TOP-sy."

> PREFERRED: BĪ-ŏp-sē
> ô-TŎP-sē

## CEREBRUM

To her cer-EB-rum Ann refers;
An empty CER-e-brum is hers.
To this conclusion I have come.
By process of my CER-e-brum.

> PREFERRED: SĔR-ə-brəm
> (This is *my* way. Some dictionaries prefer sə-RĒ-brəm.)
> Check your preferred definition below:
> CEREBRUM  1. a shallow metal vessel for holding flowers, etc.
> 2. a two-masted, gaff-rigged caravel

* Governor Al Smith of New York, children, was a candidate for the presidency of the United States on the Democratic ticket in 1928. Herbert Hoover beat him.

3. a stringed musical instrument on which the wind produces audible harmonics
4. the large rounded structure of the brain occupying most of the cranial cavity

## CHRONICLE, BRONCHIAL

The chap who says CRON-ik-l
Will also say BRONK-i-al;
But one who says CRONK-i-al
Is apt to say BRON-ik-l.

Ding dong, ding dong:
Two right, two wrong.

PREFERRED:  KRON-i-kəl
            BRŎNG-kē-əl
Check your preferred definition below:
BRONCHIAL  1. referring to the Bronx
2. comparable in size to the brontosaurus, which reached a length of sixty-five feet
3. describing a derisive or contemptuous sound made by vibrating the extended tongue and the lips while exhaling
4. of or pertaining to the windpipe

## CLANDESTINE†

I sorrow, as this bed we rest in,
That our amour must be clan-DES-tine;
But, dear illicit love of mine,
At least it isn't CLAN-des-tine.

PREFERRED:  klăn-DĔS-tən

## COUPON, BOUQUET

You say KEW-pon, meaning COOP-on?
Put your cap of nincompoop on.
Pull it tighter when you say
Bo-KAy in error for boo-KAy.

PREFERRED:  KOO-pŏn
            boo-KA

† See page 133 for the definition of clandestine.

## DOUR

Reassure
Him who's dour
At being poor.

To the Tower,
Him who's dour
(Rhyming sour)!

PREFERRED: DŌŌR

## EIGHTH

You have toped too mush, in faith;
You are shtarting on your aith.
Shorry—*eighth* izh what I mean
(I am shtarting on thirteen).

PREFERRED: ĀTTH

## ELEVEN

You say 'leven for eleven?
God may keep you out of heaven.

PREFERRED: ĭ-LEV-ən

## ELM, FILM (for teachers)

If he says ellum,
Expellum.
If he says fillum,
Killum.

PREFERRED: ĔLM, FĬLM

## EPITOME

E-PIT-o-mē is kind and fair.
Of evil EP-i-tōm beware.
Of mispronunciation he
Is clearly the e-PIT-ome.

PREFERRED: ĭ-PĬT-ə-mē
Check your preferred definition below:
EPITOME  1. shale lining a Cambrian pit
2. Essence; condensation or summary
3. refrain of a Renaissance ballad
4. and yet it does move! (Fictitiously attributed to Galileo after his recantation of the Copernican theory.)

## FEBRUARY

I was casketed to bury
In the local cemetery,
   Quite content to turn again to loam,
When the preacher said, "How very
Sad to die in Feb-yoo-ary!"—
   This rang a bell in my decaying dome.
Thought I, "Since there's no Feb-yoo-ary,
I *can't* be dead." So, blithe and merry,
   I jumped up from my coffin and went home.

PREFERRED: FĔB-rŏŏ-ĕr-ē
(But Feb-yoo-ary is coming on strong. Be sure, too, that you pronounce both r's in "library:" LĬ-brĕr-ē)

## FIGURE

Don't eat like a pig!—you're
Ruining your figure.
If you grow any bigger,
You will *have* no figger.

PREFERRED: FĬG-yər in New York, FIG-ər in London. Most American dictionaries prefer FĬG-yər, but FĬG-ər sounds fair enough to me.

## FINIS

We will not receive a minus
For pronouncing finis FĬN-is;
Still, some little devil in us
Often makes it come out FĬN-us.

PREFERRED: FĪ-nĭs

## GARAGE

Staying at the Claridge,
Sir John left his carriage
Back home in his GARāge.

Such pronunciations
Lead to wars 'twixt nations:
A well-placed barrage
Wrecked Sir John's gar-AHZH.

PREFERRED: gə-RAZH

## GENUINE

The man who speaks of JEN-yoo-īne
   Instead of JEN-yoo-in
Began a letter home, "Dear Kine":
   He had in mind "Dear Kin."

PREFERRED: JEN-yōō-ĭn

## GEOGRAPHY

Folks who say "JOG-ger-fy"
Rate no bioggerfy,
   At least not from me.
Ge-OG-ra-phy, though,
May win a bi-ó
(But no guarantee).

PREFERRED: jē-ŎG-rə-fē

## GOING TO

Sorry—owing to
   Faults I cannot stand
I'm not going to
   Sue for Mona's hand—
Not till Mona
Stops saying "gonna."

PREFERRED: GŌ-ing too

## GOVERNMENT

I didn't know quite what my chum meant,
When he exhorted, "Down with gum-ment!"
Had he said "Gov-ern-ment," who knows?
We might have downed it, I suppose.

PREFERRED:  GŬV-ərn-mənt

## WHEN -ILE FEELS -ILL

*(The words involved are listed in the left margin)*

| | |
|---|---|
| versatile | Though VER-sa-til as seasons, |
| agile | Though AJ-il as a flea, |
| fragile | And FRAJ-il, too, my dear is, |
| docile | She's DOS-il not to me. |
| sterile | I've shown that I am STER-il, and impotent, says she; |
| servile | Ah, would that she were SUR-vil, |
| | At least to a degree! |
| virile | I'd show her then how VIR-il |
| fertile | And FUR-till I could be! |
| hostile | My darling, though, is HOSS-til; |
| imbecile | She thinks me IM-be-sil. |
| futile | My love for her is FYOO-til. |
| | But it is not fyoo-TILL. |

PREFERRED:  VŬR-sə-təl
ĂJ-əl
FRĂJ-əl
DŎS-əl
STUR-əl
SUR-vəl
VĬR-əl
FURT-l
HŎS-təl
IM-bə-sĭl
FYOOT-l

(The unstressed -ile in the above words is generally pronounced -īl in Britain.)

## IGNOMINY

The boy who said "ig-NOM-in-y"
Was called up by the dom-in-ie,
Who put a dunce cap on the ninny
And sent him home in IG-no-min-y.

PREFERRED:  IG-nə-mĭn-ē

## IMPIOUS

Some IM-pi-ous old scoundrels may,
   In certain circumstances,
Get into heaven anyway;
   But don't bet on the chances
(I speak, it's true, from verbal bias)
   Of those who in the same breath boo
   God and pronunciation too
By saying they're im-PĪ-ous.

PREFERRED:  IM-pē-əs

## IMPOTENCE

I hear that IM-po-tence is tough;
Im-POT-ence must be doubly rough;
The one is punishment in hell;
The other's mispronounced as well.

PREFERRED:  ĬM-pət-ənce
(Say ĬN-fə-məs, too, not ĭn-FĀ-məs.)

## INEXORABLE

I feel for you when you complain
Of life's in-EX-or-a-ble pain.
But when you say it's in-ex-ZAWR-a-ble . . .
   That's horrible.

PREFERRED:  ĭn-ĔK-sər-ə-bəl
Check your preferred definition below:
INEXORABLE  1. unyielding; relentless
               2. unlovable
               3. stubborn
               4. strongly constructed; resistant
                  to breakage

## ITALIAN

Dog, go bite
   That old man!
He says Īt-
   alian!
Once bit,
He'll say It.

PREFERRED:  Ĭ-TAL-yən

## IT IS WHAT I

Ike, asked why
He ate mud pie,
Made reply:
" 'Swateye like."
My marlinspike
Disposed of Ike.

PREFERRED:  It ĭz hwŏt I

## MACHINATION

Machine—ma-SHĒN. Yet machination
Begins with 'mak.' Pronunciation
Is aberration.

PREFERRED:  măk-i-NĀ-shən
Check your preferred definition below:
MACHINATION
1. making by use of a machine
2. smoothing a rough or uneven surface by using a
   machine
3. the making of machinery
4. the act of plotting

## MISCHIEVOUS, GRIEVOUS

To say miss-CHĒV-i-ous
Or GRĒV-i-ous
Is not felonious—
It's just erroneous.

PREFERRED:  MIS-chə-vəs
GRĒV-əs

## MODERN, PARDON

"Be MOD-ren," says she.
Says I, "Beg your POD-ren?"
Says she, "I said MAR-den."
I still begged her PAR-don.
Said she, "Nothing's odder'n
Saying it MOD-ern."

PREFERRED:  MŎD-ərn
PÄRD-n

## ORGY

I don't think a porgy
Ever had an orgy.
A porgy's a fish,
And my guess is that for a fish an orgy
   is an unwished wish.
Anyway, porgy
Rhymes with more ghee*
While orgy
Rhymes with a disgusting
   fellow I know named Georgy.

PREFERRED:   ÔR-jē
PŌR-gē

## OUGHT TO

Slaughta
Folks who say "oughtta."

PREFERRED:   ôt tōō

## PERCOLATOR

Fella in a hash house, musta been a waiter,
Said, "We've got fresh coffee from the
   PUR-ko-lay-ter."
"It's PUR-kyoo-lay-ter, son," says I;
  "though I ain't been to school, yer
Mispronouncination I find very danged peekooliar."

The waiter was right.
Say PURK-ə-lā-tər.

## POEM

They laughed, back home,
   When I said, "Some day
I'll write a pome . . ."
  Okay, okay,
This here will show 'em.
'Tain't just a pome—
This here's a PŌ-em.

PREFERRED:   PŌ-əm
(Say also PŌ-ət not pŌT.)

* Ghee is a semifluid buffalo butter made chiefly in India.

# PREFERABLE

It is preferable to
Say PREF-er-able. Ach, mon dyoo!
    Pr-e-FUR-able
    Sounds turrible.

PREFERABLE:   PRĔF-ər-ə-bəl
ALSO PREFERABLE:   CŎM-pər-ə-bəl
       AM-ĭ-kə-bəl
       DĔS-pĭ-kə-bəl
       RĔP-yə-tə-bəl
       ĂP-lĭ-kə-bəl
       ĔKS-plĭ-kə-bəl
       LĂM-ən-tə-bəl
       HŎS-pə-tə-bəl

# PROBABLY

"I'm a poor blea—
    The part of a tree
        Next to the bark."
        ". . . Blea?"
            "[*Sob!*] Blea.
                You prob'ly
    Never will see
        Me here in the dark."
"Blea, the word's PROB-a-bly."
"Say, then, I'm [*sob!*] a blea—
        Probably
        [*Sob!*] a blea
            Ever unseen.
    Pray strip my bark away;
    Then I can lark away
            Gay as a queen.
    Since I'm just [*sob!*] a blea,
    You'll leave me, probably . . .
    Wait, sir, come back to me! . . .
            See what I mean?"

PREFERABLE:   PRŎB-ə-blē

# QUAY

A quay's pronounced like key: some day
I'll find the quay to winning Kay.

PREFERRED: KĒ
Check your preferred definition below:
QUAY  1. the general pitch or tone of the speaking voice
2. an artificial landing place for loading or unloading vessels
3. an instrument, usually metal, for shooting or drawing the bolt of a lock
4. the bow of a vessel, below the water line

## RECOGNIZE

If you hear a man who cries
"RECK-er-nize" for "REC-og-nize,"
You should rec-og-nize that he
Is not fit for com-pa-ny.

PREFERRED: RĔK-əg-nīz

## RIBALD

Once, astride a pony pie-bald,
Much rye whiskey having high-balled,
I in swaying saddle scribbled
Certain verses sad but RIB-ald
(Notice I do not say RĪb-ald)
While a tear-ball from my eye-ball d-ribbled.

PREFERRED: RIB-əld
Check your preferred definition below:
RIBALD  1. rib-tickling; hilarious
2. low, coarse, or scurrilous
3. relating to a disease of the cartilaginous rods which stiffen the lateral walls of the body
4. semi-bald; suffering loss of hair

## SATURDAY

(Addie speaking:)
My lovin' sugar daddy
    Talks right;
When I'm speakin' bad, he
    Turns white.
My lovin' sugar daddy
Asked me to his paddy
To eat finnan haddie.

I says, "Sure—nex' *Saddy?*"
He says, "Never, Addie.
No more sugar daddy,
No more daddy's paddy,
No more finnan haddie,
Never, never, Addie.
    Good *night*."

PREFERRED:  SĂT-ər-dā

## SECRETIVE

My neighbor John, who cheats,
   Is cheative.
What's Suzy, who secretes?
   SeCRĒT-ive.
(Though some forgive
   SĒC-re-tive.)

PREFERRED:  sə-CRET-iv

## SLOUGH

I do not know, or care, if you
    Rhyme "slough" with "goo."
Nor do I give a hoot if thou
    Rhyme'st "slough" with "cow."
But I know anybody
Who falls in one gets muddy.

PREFERRED:  For slough, defined as a mire, either "slōo" or "slou": For slough, defined as a discarded skin, or as a verb meaning to shed a skin, "slŭf."

## STATUS

"Status" doesn't rhyme with "pat us"—
That's a barbarism, that is—
But, correctly rhymed with "hate us,"
Shows superior social status.

PREFERRED:  STĀ-təs

## THEATER

I saw her through a magic prism
Till she called theater "thē-Ā-ter."

Lest she repeat that solecism,
  I boiled her in a mechanism,
    And ate her.

PREFERRED: THĒ-ə-tər

## VAGARY

Until his second lager, he
Considers drink a VA-ga-ry;
But later on, when mellow-merry,
Says *not* to drink is the va-GĀ-ry.

PREFERRED: It's a toss-up. I say və-GĀR-ē,<br>but if you insist on VĀ-gər-ē, I'll say it your<br>way.

## VANILLA

I know a fella
Who says vi-NELL-a.
Isn't that silla?
He means va-NILL-a.

PREFERRED: və-nĭl-ə

## ZOOLOGY

Although
The zoo
Is where
We see
The bear,
The gnu,
The chickadee—
When we explore
These creatures, we
Don't call the chore
Zoo-ology.
Zō-ol-o-gy is right, although
The reason why I do not know.

PREFERRED: zō-ŎL-ə-jē

VERSES TO IMPROVE
YOUR USAGE

## AIN'T I (a triolet)

My tongue can't handle "Amn't I"—
   I'm going back to "Ain't I."
Though "Am I not" is stiff and dry,
My tongue can't handle "Amn't I";
And as to "Aren't I"—I may try
   To shun that horror, mayn't I?
My tongue can't handle "Amn't I"—
   I'm going back to "Ain't I."

## ALRIGHT'S NOT ALL RIGHT

By day and night
 I sing this song:
"All right's all right;
 Alright's all wrong."

   Alright is never acceptable English.

## ALL READY, ALREADY

 Said Mary to Eddy,
"Let's turn down the beddy."
"No reason to," said he
  (The "he" meaning Eddy):
"The beddy's *already*
   All ready."
   (So's Eddy.)

   Already is an adverb referring to a completed action. All ready
means "everything [or everyone] ready." It is right to say, "He is
already in school, and all ready for his first class." It would be
equally right to say, "He is all ready for school. He is already in his
first class."

## ALL TOGETHER, ALTOGETHER

Dear comrades, let us all together to the barman cry
That we for lack of beer and gin are altogether dry.
Then let us all together hoist the brimming, cheering cup;
Till we fall all together,
                Altogether bottoms-up.

All together means "everyone at once," or "everyone in the same location." Altogether means "completely."

| | | |
|---|---|---|
| WRONG: | We are altogether again. |
| RIGHT: | We are all together again. |
| WRONG: | He is all together in error. |
| RIGHT: | He is altogether in error. |

## AWFUL, AWFULLY

If you say awful
  A lot,
By me it's lawful—
  Why not?
But DON'T say "awful good" (or bad)
For awful then becomes an ad-
verb, forcing it to be
Stretched on the rack to aw-ful-ly.

Awful once meant awe-inspiring. Informally, it has become an intensive: "That boy shows an awful lot of sense." The usage is informal: if you are addicted to it, at least distinguish between the adjective and the adverb.

## BALANCE, REMAINDER

The first part of April, it rained.
  The balance was dreadfully dry.
(Excuse me: not balance; remaind-
  er; balance is something I try
To keep in my bank. It's ordained
  That for the remainder of my
Existence, I'll be in the red;
  On balance, I'd rather be dead.)

Though balance has other meanings, it is acceptable as a synonym for remainder only in reference to financial transactions or records. You can speak correctly of your "cash balance," but not of the "balance of your vacation."

## BETWEEN, AMONG

When I was asked to choose *between*
Roberta, Ethel, and Eileen,
My curt refusal may have stung them—
But I could only choose *among* them.
(Between us two, 'twas just as well;
The girl I love is Isabelle.)

The rule is: Between two; among more than two.

> RIGHT: We divided the marbles *among* Joe, Bill, and John.
> Mary and I settled our quarrel *between* ourselves.

## BETWEEN YOU AND I

Unique, you say,
This passion be-
tween you and I,
Between we two—
I and you.

Dear love, pooh-pooh:
We have no way
To quantify
The passion be-
tween he and she—
Them and they.

"Between you and I (we, he, she, they)" for "between you and me (him, her, us, them)" is outrageous.

## BRING, TAKE

Bring moves toward you. Take moves off:

I'll bring you a bottle of prime Beaujolais;
But if you refuse me, I'll take it away.

## CAPABLE, ABLE

Capable and able one may justly interchange
As meaning "with capacity to do, perform, arrange."
Yet capable is able to accept the passive voice,
While able isn't capable of making such a choice.
I'm capable of hammering; I'm able, too, to hammer;
Of being hammered, capable; and yet, so silly's grammar,
Not able. Foolish rules like these are often inescapable;
You can't be more confused than I. This makes us both
    incapable.

> WRONG: This gun is able to be fired.
> RIGHT: This gun is capable of being fired.

## CONVINCE TO

The day the man who seeks to justify
Convince to can convince me I should say
Convince to—that, dear sir, will be the day
That I'm convinced to finalize my stay,
Existence-wise, upon this ball of clay:
>  That is to say,
>> The day
>>> I
>>>> Die.

I am an easygoing chap, and tend to avoid hopeless fights. To object to convince to is a hopeless fight; I checked off the phrase one morning thirty-three times in the New York *Times,* and doubtless would have found it as many times more if I had continued turning the pages. I have even seen it in William Safire's column. But I will fight convince to till my last breath. It is not only wrong, not only inexcusable, but aesthetically revolting. I sum up my case in the words of an expert witness—the late Theodore M. Bernstein, for years the usage czar of that same New York *Times:*

> The distinction between these words is clear, but not to everyone. *Convince* means to get someone to believe something and *persuade* means to get someone to do something. . . . For that reason *persuade* may be followed by an infinitive: "The police *persuaded* the robber *to drop* his gun." *Convince,* on the other hand, should never be followed by an infinitive. It may be followed by an *of* phrase or a *that* clause: "The police *convinced* the robber *of* the hopelessness of holding out" or "The police *convinced* the robber *that* his situation was hopeless." If you are *convinced of* the difference between these two words, perhaps you will be *persuaded* never *to use* an infinitive after *convince.*

But I have given up trying to convince you to change. I no longer go beyond saying "Shame on you."

*Dangling Modifiers:*

> When a word, phrase, or clause hangs loosely within a sentence, so that it does not refer clearly and logically to some other word, it is said to dangle. A sentence with a dangling modifier is incoherent; one understands it only by a leap of intuition.

# DANGLE, DANGLE, LITTLE STRAY

Dangle, dangle, little stray!
How I wonder what you say!
In all reason, there is sure to
Be *some* phrase that you refer to:
"On a walk, the sun sank low" . . .
"Sitting, it began to snow" . . .
"When a boy, my father took me" . . .
"When a girl, my mother shook me" . . .
"Stir the mixture till dark tan" . . .
"Standing up, the hymn began" . . .

Dangle, dangle, little stray!
How I wonder what you say!

# DATA, DATUM

Data are not singular;
Data are not is but are—
    The singular is datum.
When opponents say to you,
"Data backs my point of view,"
    Do as I do—hate 'em.

A datum is a granted fact. Data are more than one datum.

# EACH OTHER, ONE ANOTHER

In formal speech, say "each other" when two persons are involved, but "one another" when there are more than two. In informal speech, forget it.

A maxim once true—
Each other for two;
For more, one another—
Has gone up the flue:
One another, each other—
Either other will do.

Still, if you prefer to be technical:

Brothers twain combat each other;
Brothers three fight one another.
It's hard upon the brothers' mother.

## EAGER, ANXIOUS

Though Cal's appetite is meager,
For our whiskey Cal is eager.
When he shtaggersh up and thanksh us,
We're not eager—we are anxious.

To be eager is to be ardently desirous; to be anxious is to be worried and troubled.

## FEWER, LESS

I wish that my troubles were fewer;
  I wish that my troubles were less;
Fewer, the woes I endure;
  Less, their unbearableness.

Few means "not many"; little means "not much." Fewer means "smaller in number"; less means "smaller in amount," as in "I have fewer legs than a centipede, but a centipede has less intelligence." (A doubtful proposition.)

## FORMER, LATTER: FIRST, LAST

Former, latter, are in sum
  But two; while first and last
Embrace between them all to come
  And all forever past.

When speaking of only two objects or ideas, refer to the former or latter, not to the first or last. Use first and last when more than two are involved.

## ILL, WELL; BAD, GOOD

When you're ill,
You're not well;
When you're bad,
You're not good.
Thus you use
These words, Estelle—
Or thus you should.

Ill (adjective). Diseased; in bad health. An ill child child stays in bed.

Ill (adverb). In an ill manner; badly; wickedly. He, being a little more drunk than usual, behaved extremely ill.

Well (adverb). In a good or proper manner; satisfactorily. You did *well*.

Well (adjective). Healthy. A well child runs and plays.

Good (adjective). Not bad; proper, right; benevolent. You are a good dog.

"I feel good" as a description of one's health is unacceptable; "I feel well" is right. Well can be either an adjective or an adverb, while good is only an adjective.

## INCREASINGLY MORE

"Increasingly more"
 I abhor.
 I press
For "increasingly less."

Not really. But the former redundancy is as common among college professors as among cab drivers—more common, since cab drivers are not in the habit of saying "increasingly."

## MORE

Jim asked her, "Do you love me more
   Than Harrison?"
      Said she:
"Say first how much he loves you, for
   Comparison."
      Said he:
"I mean, dear, do you love me more than—"
      Then she:
   "Him, or he?
If he, it's 'more than he loves me';
If him, it's 'more than I love him.'
But I am only having fun—
I love you, dear, not Harrison."

"I love you more than Harrison" could mean either, "I love you more than I love Harrison," or "I love you more than Harrison loves you." Be clear in your statements, especially if you are in love.

## IT IS I, IT IS ME

It's safe to dis-re-gard the guy
Who with pre-cis-ion says "It's I";
"It's me" has clearly won the day
(In conversation, anyway).
But do not challenge him to fight,
For tech-ni-cal-ly he is right.

"It is I," "It is we," "It is he," "It is she," "It is they" are all unas-
sailable; when "to be" has no subject, its complement is in the sub-
jective case. But here usage has grammar on the run. In informal
speech, these locutions sound affected.

## THE OWL THAT SAYS "TO-WHIT, TO-WHO"

The owl that says "to-whit, to-who,"
 Grammaticists agree,
Should say "to-whom," and so should you.
 And so should me.

Were you a German-speaking Serb,
 You might well ask, *"Warum\**
Is 'who' the subject of a verb,
 The object being 'whom'."

To which, were I Italián,
 And Doris Day's mamá,
I'd say, "Use either as you can,
 For *que sera, sera.*"

## LOAN, LEND†

Though loan's a noun (the verb is lend),
 Care not should someone note that you
Say "Loan friend money and lose friend."
 So all your neighbors use "loan," too.
 Besides, the saying's true.

Loan has won acceptance as a verb except in the most formal
conversation. It has established itself also in the written language.
You will sound odd (except in England) if you *don't* use it.

---

\* "Why" in German.
One says, "Whom did you see?" but "Who saw you?" The usage becomes
complicated in such sentences as "I did not see whoever committed the felony."
Whoever, not whomever, is correct here; it is the subject of the verb "committed."
The entire clause "whoever committed the felony" is the object of the verb "see."
† See also "Rise, and Raise."

# MAJORITY, PLURALITY

If you and Oates
  Should vie for votes,
And you should wind
  Up behind—
Oates won his vic-tor-y
By a ma-jor-i-ty.

If Bill LaRue
  Was running too,
And Bill should get more votes
Than you, and more than Oates
(But less than both of you)
Bill won his vic-tor-y
By a plur-al-i-ty
(And may, the sly old fox,
Have stuffed the ballot box).

If two people are running for office, the winner must get more than half of the votes—a *majority*. If more than two people are running, the winner is the one who gets more votes than any of the others—a *plurality*. If A, B, and C are running for office, A's 40 per cent of the votes will win by a plurality if B has 35 per cent and C 25 per cent.

## MAY, CAN

Generally, if you may, you have permission to; if you can, you have the ability to. For instance:

I may do what you ban not,
  Assuming that I can.
  There's no need to ban
  The evil things a man
Wants to do, but cannot.

Can here delivers a biological rather than a grammatical message:

"Can I become a man?" asks little Bill.
  I answer, "More than that, my lad; you will."
Jane asks, "And me?" I offer a suggestion:
  "Rephrase the question."

In "A flower can or may be red," can and may are interchangeable. May, however, also means "choose to," as in the last
line of the quatrain below:

> The English neigh, in voices gay,
> "Hooray, hooray, the first of May,
> Something or other begins today!"
> What is that something or other, pray?
> I may not tell you; or else I may.

## MEMORANDA, MEMORANDUM

> When I was boss, I canned a
>   Well-intentioned man
> Who wrote more memoranda
>   Than I had time to scan.
>     I canned 'm
>     By memorandum.

## NEITHER (ONE): EACH (ONE)
(a rondel in thirteen lines)

> Unless you weed the pathways neural
>   Connecting verb and noun,
> You'll find that singular and plural
>   Grow often upside down.
>
> Shun "Neither of his dogs *are* brown,"
>   For *one*'s implicit; speech is puerile‡
> Unless you weed the pathways neural
>   Connecting verb and noun.
>
> In urban sprawl or hamlet rural,
>   Say never, "Each of us go down."
> The subject's *one* still. There's no cure-all
> Unless you weed the pathways neural
>   Connecting verb and noun.

In "Neither of his dogs," *one* is clearly understood between "neither" and "of." One takes a singular verb. The same reasoning
applies to "each of us," "everyone," etc.

## ONLY

> He said that he loved only me;
>   I would I could believe him.

‡ Some say puer-Ile.

He said that only he loved me;
  I did not undeceive him.
He loved me—only that said he;
  I wished he'd further spoken;
Since only he said he loved me
(And pledge that has no warranty
  Is pledge that's easy broken)
  I needed other token.
He said he only loved me. Bliss!
Heart could not compass more than this.

For clear conversation, as for clear writing, keep your modifier close to the word being modified. Of the protestations above, the first affirms that the lover loves but the one girl; the second, that she is loved by no one else; the third, that his profession of love is as far as he is ready to go; the fourth, that even this profession remains unconfirmed; the fifth, that she can expect nothing from him but his love.

## QUICK, SLOW: QUICKLY, SLOWLY

Cries wife, "Go quick!" Cries wife, "Go slow!"
Replies superior husband, "No,
  Dear; quick and slow are adjectives.
Your verb needs adverbs: quickly, slowly."

  Whatever your good spouse believes,
Ma'am, stand your ground, by all that's holy!
These adjectives to adverbs vary,
As shown in any dictionary.

I quote the following monstrosity from a textbook by a respected professor of English:

*Quick-quickly*

"Quick" is an adjective; "quickly" is an adverb. *Wrong:* He worked quick in order to avoid detection. (Wrong because the adverbial form is needed to modify the verb "worked.")

The professor wrote wrong and wrongly. Wrong, like quick, slow, well, and ill, is either an adjective or an adverb, according to its use.

### LIE, LAY (a virelay)

Lie down once more where once we kissed,
   While I the laws of lie and lay
Lay down. Where lay we, lie—and list,
   Here where you lay and lied, dear Kay:
Lie down once more where once we kissed.

Here where a hundred lads had lain,
   You swore to lie with me for aye.
You laid sweet ambush to my brain;
   You lay; lied; laid one more lad prey
Here where a hundred lads had lain.

Lie. To recline. Takes no object. Past tense, lay. Past participle, lain. Present participle, lying. I am going to lie down. Last night I lay down. We have lain down. We are lying down.

Lie. To tell an untruth. Takes no object. Past tense, lied. Past participle, lied. Present participle, lying. You lie, you lied, you have lied, you are lying.

Lay. To place, to set. Always takes an object. Past tense, laid. Past participle, laying. Present participle, laying. I lay the pencil on the paper. I laid the pencil on the paper. I have laid the pencil on the paper. I am laying the pencil on the paper.

### RISE, RAISE

The worker striking for a rise
   Who winds up with a raise,
Will find the money gratifies,
   Whatever grammar says.
Raise is a verb, and rise a noun,
   And so you should employ them;
But don't knock dollars raining down—
   Relax; enjoy them.

Raise is not really a noun, but a verb that takes an object, as in "raise a ruckus." But raise used as a noun for an increase in wage or salary is so pervasive that it would be quixotic to deny that it has become standard English (except in England). If you can't lick 'em, j'in 'em.

## SET, SIT

We test all rules (so goes the wheeze)
By their irregularities.

"Set" takes an object; "sit" does not.
We set a fire beneath a pot;
We sit and dream beneath the trees.

Yet ponder these anomalies:

It's quite acceptable to say
"The sun will set at eight today" . . .
"My mind is set" . . . "The old red hen
Is setting on her eggs again."

If in your ways you're set, my pet,
Be set, be set . . . be not too set.

There are other exceptions to the rule that "set" must take an object. It is all right, for instance, to say that you are "setting out on a trip," or that the current is "setting westward." But if you say, "He sets down" for "He sits down," or "He set down" for "He sat down," or, "He sat his plane down" for "He set his plane down," you will be branded, rightly or wrongly, an ignoramus.

## SUPINE, PRONE

When stomping foe recumbent,
    Attack the proper zone:
The belly if he's supine,
    The back if he is prone.

It is hard to understand how "supine" and "prone" could have become so generally confused. "Supine" is from Latin *supinus,* "backward, lying on one's back." "Prone," from Latin *pronus,* "inclined forward," means lying with the face downward, "the opposite," says my dictionary, "of supine." Yet only the other day I read in a book by a respected and presumably literate author, "He lay prone upon his back."

## UNINTERESTED, DISINTERESTED

I'm an ancient one:
I'm completely *un-*
interested in
Adolescent sin—

Say a furtive kiss.
Coolly I compare
Kiss of Kate and Clare,
Judging them with *dis-*
interest.

     Hmmm . . . This
One's sweeter, I declare.


Uninterested means indifferent. Disinterested means unbiased, impartial.

## WILL, SHALL

One alternates at will (or shall;
  Do you perceive my little jest?),
In idle chat, 'twixt shall and will.
  For formal speech, though, it were best
To memorize a certain drill
  That shall and will turns quite about,
Lets each one in where it was out,
  Turns ill to well, and well to ill.

In simple future we descry
  Unalterable time pass by:
"Next year I shall be twenty-such;
  They, you, he, she, will be so much."

But promise or determination
  At once capsizes the equation;
"I will succeed; who bars my path
  Shall feel the hammer of my wrath."

For simple futurity, the forms are:

     I shall, you will, he (she, it), will.
     We shall, you will, they will.

For determination or promise, the order is reversed:

     I will, you shall, he (she, it) shall.

This was true, at least, until the Irish came along in the nineteenth century.

# UNCERTAIN? DIAL (501) 569-3162

If you are unsure about the acceptability of a word or phrase, dial (501) 569-3162.

According to United Press International, (501) 569-3162 is the number of a hot line for grammar emergencies at the University of Arkansas, Little Rock. It is at your service between 9 A.M. and noon (presumably Little Rock time) every day except Saturday and Sunday.

The hot line is the creation of Dr. Stuart Peterfreund, assistant professor of English at the university. When the UPI story appeared, his office was receiving up to seventy-five calls a day, explaining such distinctions as that between affect and effect, or, for all I know, between insist and incest.

If a Russian answers, hang up. You tapped the President's hot line.

# APPENDIX I

*Alphabetical review of words covered in the pronunciation verses. Check your choices below. You will see on pages 203–4 how many words you have said my way, and whether, by my standards, your pronunciation is below average, average, good, or excellent.*

Your choice

| | | | | |
|---|---|---|---|---|
| 1. ACCEDE | A. ăk-SĒD | B. ăss-SĒD | A__ B__ |
| 2. ACCEPT | A. ăk-SĔPT | B. ăss-SĔPT | A__ B__ |
| 3. ACCESSORY | A. ăss-SĔS-əry | B. ăk-SĔS-əry | A__ B__ |
| 4. AGILE | A. ĂJ-īl | B. ĂJ-əl | A__ B__ |
| 5. ATHLETE | A. ĂTH-lēt | B. ĂTH-e-lēt | A__ B__ |
| 6. ATTACKED | A. ə-TĂKTED | B. ə-TĂKT | A__ B__ |
| 7. AUTOPSY | A. Ô-top-sē | B. ô-TŎP-sē | A__ B__ |
| 8. AVIATOR | A. Ā-vē-āt-ər | B. ĂV-ē-āt-ər | A__ B__ |
| 9. AWRY | A. aw-RȲE | B. aw-REE | A__ B__ |
| 10. BICYCLE | A. BĪ-sī-kəl | B. BĪ-sĭk-əl | A__ B__ |
| 11. BIOPSY | A. BĪ-ŏp-sē | B. bī-OP-sē | A__ B__ |
| 12. BOUQUET | A. bō-KĀ | B. boͦo-KĀ | A__ B__ |
| 13. BRONCHIAL | A. BRŎNG-kē-əl | B. BRON-ək-əl | A__ B__ |
| 14. CEREBRUM | A. SĔR-ə-brəm | B. sēr-ĒB-rəm | A__ B__ |
| 15. CHLORINE | A. KLOR-in | B. KLOR-ēn | A__ B__ |
| 16. CHRONICLE | A. KRON-i-kəl | B. KRONK-ial | A__ B__ |
| 17. CLANDESTINE | A. KLĂN-dĕs-tīn | B. klăn-DĔS-tən | A__ B__ |
| 18. CONSUMMATE | A. (v.) cŏn-sə-MĀT | B. con-SUM-mət | A__ B__ |
| 19.       " | A. (adj.) cən-SUM-ət | B. cən-sum-māt | A__ B__ |
| 20. COUPON | A. KEW-pŏn | B. KOͦO-pŏn | A__ B__ |
| 21. DEBOUCH | A. dĕ-BOUCH | B. dĕ-BOOSH | A__ B__ |
| 22. DOCILE | A. DŎS-īl | B. DŎS-əl | A__ B__ |
| 23. DOUR | A. DOWR | B. DOͦOR | A__ B__ |
| 24. EIGHTH | A. ĀTTH | B. ĀTH | A__ B__ |
| 25. ELEVEN | A. ĕ-LEV-ən | B. LEV-ən | A__ B__ |
| 26. ELM | A. ELL-um | B. ĔLM | A__ B__ |
| 27. EPITOME | A. ĕ-PĬT-ə-mē | B. EP-i-tōm | A__ B__ |
| 28. FEBRUARY | A. FĔB-roͦo-ĕr-ē | B. FEB-yoͦo-ĕr-ē | A__ B__ |
| 29. FERTILE | A. FURT-l | B. FURT-īl | A__ B__ |
| 30. FIGURE | A. FĬG-yər | B. FIG-ər | A__ B__ |
| 31. FILM | A. FĬLM | B. FILL-um | A__ B__ |
| 32. FINIS | A. FĬN-ĭs | B. FĪN-ĭs | A__ B__ |
| 33. FRAGILE | A. FRĂJ-əl | B. FRĂJ-īl | A__ B__ |
| 34. FUTILE | A. FYOͦOT-l | B. FYOͦO-tīl | A__ B__ |
| 35. GARAGE | A. GAR-əj | B. gə-RĂZH | A__ B__ |
| 36. GENUINE | A. JEN-yoͦo-īn | B. JEN-yoͦo-ĭn | A__ B__ |
| 37. GEOGRAPHY | A. jē-ŎG-rə-fē | B. JOG-ər-fē | A__ B__ |
| 38. GOVERNMENT | A. GŬV-ərn-mənt | B. GUV-mənt | A__ B__ |
| 39. GRAMERCY | A. gram-ERC-y | B. GRAM-erc-y | A__ B__ |
| 40. GRIEVOUS | A. GRĒV-əs | B. GRĒV-ē-əs | A__ B__ |
| 41. HOSTILE | A. HŎS-tīl | B. HŎS-təl | A__ B__ |
| 42. IGNOMINY | A. ig-NOM-in-ē | B. IG-nə-mĭn-ē | A__ B__ |

| 43. IMBECILE | A. IM-bə-sĭl | B. IM-bə-sīl | A__ B__ |
|---|---|---|---|
| 44. IMPIOUS | A. IM-pē-əs | B. im-PĪ-əs | A__ B__ |
| 45. IMPOTENCE | A. im-PŌT-ənce | B. ĬM-pət-ənce | A__ B__ |
| 46. INDEFATIGIBLE | A. in-di-fa-TĒ-ga-bəl | B. in-dĭ-FĂT-ə-ga-bəl | A__ B__ |
| 47. INEXORABLE | A. ĭn-ex-ZAWR-ə-bəl | B. ĭn-ĔK-ser-ə-bəl | A__ B__ |
| 48. INFAMOUS | A. ĭn-FĀ-məs | B. ĬN-fə-məs | A__ B__ |
| 49. ITALIAN | A. Ĭ-TĂL-yən | B. Ĭ-TĂL-yən | A__ B__ |
| 50. LIBRARY | A. LĬ-brĕr-ē | B. LĬ-bĕr-ē | A__ B__ |
| 51. MACHINATION | A. MĂK-in-ā-shən | B. MASH-in-ā-shən | A__ B__ |
| 52. MISCHIEVOUS | A. mis-CHĒ-vəs | B. MIS-chə-vəs | A__ B__ |
| 53. MODERN | A. MŎD-ərn | B. MOD-rən | |
| | | C. MAR-dən | A__ B__ C__ |
| 54. MOTORCYCLE | A. MŌT-ər-sĭk-əl | B. MŌT-ər-SĪ-kəl | A__ B__ |
| 55. ORGY | A. ÔR-jē | B. ÔR-ghē | A__ B__ |
| 56. PARDON | A. POD-ren | B. PÄRD-n | A__ B__ |
| 57. PERCOLATOR | A. PURK-ə-lā-tər | B. PER-kū-lā-tər | A__ B__ |
| 58. PICTURE | A. PIK-chər | B. PITCH-ər | A__ B__ |
| 59. PITCHER | A. PIK-chər | B. PITCH-ər | A__ B__ |
| 60. POEM | A. PŌ-əm | B. PŌM | A__ B__ |
| 61. POSTHUMOUS | A. PŎS-choͦo-məs | B. pos-CHOO-məs | A__ B__ |
| 62. PREFERABLE | A. pre-FUR-ə-bəl | B. PRĔF-er-ə-bəl | A__ B__ |
| 63. PROBABLY | A. PRŌ-blē | B. PRŎB-ə-blē | A__ B__ |
| 64. QUAY | A. KĒ | B. KĀ | A__ B__ |
| 65. RADIATOR | A. RĀ-dē-ā-tər | B. RĂD-ē-ā-tər | A__ B__ |
| 66. RADIO | A. RĀ-dē-ō | B. RĂD-ē-ō | A__ B__ |
| 67. RECOGNIZE | A. RĔK-əg-nīz | B. REK-ə-nīz | A__ B__ |
| 68. RIBALD | A. RĪ-bəld | B. RĬB-əld | A__ B__ |
| 69. SATURDAY | A. SĂD-dā | B. SĂT-ər-dā | A__ B__ |
| 70. SECRETIVE | A. SĒC-re-tiv | B. sə-CRĒT-iv | A__ B__ |
| 71. SERVILE | A. SUR-vəl | B. SUR-vīl | A__ B__ |
| 72. SLOUGH (to shed) | A. SLOͦO | B. SLŬF | A__ B__ |
| 73. STATUS | A. STĂT-us | B. STĀ-təs | A__ B__ |
| 74. STERILE | A. STĔR-əl | B. STĔR-īl | A__ B__ |
| 75. SUCCINCT | A. sək-SINGKT | B. səss-SINGKT | A__ B__ |
| 76. THEATER | A. THĒ-ə-tər | B. thē-AY-tər | A__ B__ |
| 77. UNICYCLE | A. yoͦo-nĭ-SĪ-kəl | B. YOͦO-nĭ-sĭk-əl | A__ B__ |
| 78. VAGARY | A. VĀ-gər-ē | B. və-GĀR-ē | A__ B__ |
| 79. VANILLA | A. və-NĬL-ə | B. vin-ELL-ə | A__ B__ |
| 80. VERSATILE | A. VÛR-sə-təl | B. VÛR-sə-tīl | A__ B__ |
| 81. VIRILE | A. VĬR-īl | B. VĬR-əl | A__ B__ |
| 82. ZOOLOGY | A. zoͦo-Ŏl-ə-je | B. zo-ŎL-ə-jē | A__ B__ |

### KEY TO PROPER PRONUNCIATION

| WORD | | WORD | | WORD | | WORD | | WORD | | WORD | |
|---|---|---|---|---|---|---|---|---|---|---|---|
| 1. | A | 9. | A | 17. | B | 25. | A | 33. | A | 41. | B |
| 2. | A | 10. | B | 18. | A | 26. | B | 34. | A | 42. | B |
| 3. | B | 11. | A | 19. | A | 27. | A | 35. | B | 43. | A |
| 4. | B | 12. | B | 20. | B | 28. | A | 36. | B | 44. | A |
| 5. | A | 13. | A | 21. | B | 29. | A | 37. | A | 45. | B |
| 6. | B | 14. | A | 22. | B | 30. | A | 38. | A | 46. | B |
| 7. | B | 15. | B | 23. | B | 31. | A | 39. | A | 47. | B |
| 8. | A | 16. | A | 24. | A | 32. | A | 40. | A | 48. | B |

| WORD | | WORD | | WORD | | WORD | | WORD | | WORD | |
|---|---|---|---|---|---|---|---|---|---|---|---|
| 49. | A | 55. | A | 61. | A | 67. | A | 73. | B | 78. | A or B |
| 50. | A | 56. | B | 62. | B | 68. | B | 74. | A | 79. | A |
| 51. | A | 57. | A | 63. | B | 69. | B | 75. | A | 80. | A |
| 52. | B | 58. | A | 64. | A | 70. | B | 76. | A | 81. | B |
| 53. | A | 59. | B | 65. | A | 71. | A | 77. | A | 82. | B |
| 54. | A | 60. | A | 66. | A | 72. | B | | | | |

75 to 82 correct answers is excellent; 65 to 74 is above average; 55 to 64 is average. Remember that you are measuring yourself simply against *my* preferences; dictionaries accept more than one pronunciation for many of these words.

# APPENDIX II

An alphabetical list of the 181 words covered in the vocabulary and pronunciation/vocabulary verses.

Abbreviations of source languages:

| G. | Greek |
|---|---|
| MG. | Middle Greek |
| L. | Latin |
| ML. | Middle Latin |
| NL. | New Latin |
| AS. | Anglo-Saxon |
| Ger. | German |
| LS. | Low Scotch |
| Sca. | Scandinavian |
| Da. | Danish |
| ME. | Middle English |
| F. | French |
| Sp. | Spanish |
| It. | Italian |
| OF. | Old French |
| OHG. | Old High German |
| MLG. | Middle Low German |
| Heb. | Hebrew |
| Ic. | Icelandic |
| Mal. | Malay |
| H. | Hindu |

CORRECT DEFINITIONS

ABATE
1. [L. *batere*, to beat]; to lower in force or intensity. "My fury shall abate, and I the crowns will take." (Shakespeare)

ACUITY
1. [L. *acuo*, to sharpen]; sharpness (of mind).

ADDLED
4. [AS. *adl*, a disease, *adela*, filth]; unsound or confused, as brains; muddled. "My muddy brain is addled like an egg." (Fielding)

ADOLESCENT
4. [L. *adolescere*, to grow up]; like a teen-ager; pertaining to the time between childhood and maturity.

| ADULTEROUS | 4. | [L. *adulterare*, to adulterate]; related to or given to illicit sexual relations, esp. in transgression of marriage. |
| AFFLUENCE | 4. | [L. *affluere*, to flow to]; abundance of property, wealth, profusion. "They lived in affluence." (Steele) |
| AFTERMATH | 3. | [AS. *aefter*, after, behind+*maeth*, to cut]; figuratively, consequences, esp. disastrous consequences. |
| AGGRANDIZE | 3. | [L. *aggrandir*, *a*, to+*grandir*, to increase]; to make great; to enlarge; increase. "The scene, though small, is yet aggrandized with much art." (Miller) |
| AGILE | 4. | [L. *agere*, to move]; having the faculty of quick, dexterous, and easy motion; deftly nimble; active; also mentally quick. |
| ALTRUISTIC | 1. | [F. *autre*, other]; pertaining to regard for, and devotion to, the interests of others as an ethical principle; unselfish. |
| AMUCK, AMOK | 3. | [Mal. *amok*, furious attack]; in a frenzy to do violence or kill. "Satire's my weapon, but I'm too discreet to run amuck." (Pope) |
| ANACHRONISTIC | 3. | [G. *ana*, backward, reversed+*khronizein*, to belong to a particular time]; existing or happening at other than its proper or historical time. |
| ANATHEMA | 3. | [G. *anathema*, a votive offering devoted to destruction]; an imprecation; curse; malediction. "Finally she fled to London followed by the anathemas of both families." (Thackeray) |
| ANESTHETIC | 4. | [G. *anaisthetos*, want of feeling]; a temporary duller of pain. |
| ANIMUS | 1. | [L. *animus*, mind, soul]; a feeling of animosity; bitter hostility; hatred. ". . . with an often ill-concealed animus." (Edel) |
| ANOMALOUS | 2. | [G. *an*, not+*homalos*, even]; deviating from the normal or common order, form, or rule; abnormal; deviant. |
| ANONYMOUS | 2. | [G. *a*, without+*onoma*, name]; nameless. "Nearly a hundred years have passed since an anonymous benefactor founded in France a prize for virtue." *Daily News*, August 3, 1878. |
| APATHETIC | 4. | [G. *apatheia*, *a*, not+*patheia*, feeling]; listless; void of feeling. "He wept himself into a state of apathetic tranquillity." (Trollope) |
| APOTHEGM | 4. | [G. *apophthegma*, thing uttered]; a short, pithy, and instructive saying; a maxim. |
| ARDOR | 3. | [L. *ardere*, to burn]; warmth or heat of passion or affection; eagerness; zeal; enthusiasm. ". . . adventurous ardor, nobly triumphing." (Browning) |
| ASSIGNATION | 4. | [L. *assignare*, assign]; appointment, esp. a tryst between lovers. |
| ATHEIST | 3. | [G. *a*, absence of, without+*theos*, God]; disbelief in a God. "It is true that a little philosophy inclineth man's mind to atheism, but depth in philosophy bringeth men's minds about to religion." (Bacon) |
| ATTRIBUTE | 2. | [L. *attribuere*, to allot, grant]; a quality considered as belonging to or inherent in a person or thing; a distinctive feature, characteristic. "Mercy is . . . an attribute of God himself." (Shakespeare) |

| | | |
|---|---|---|
| AUDACIOUS | 4. | [L. *audere*, to dare, be eager]; fearlessly daring; bold, adventurous; lacking restraint or circumspection. "Audacious cruelty." (Shakespeare) |
| AWRY | 2. | [F., AS. *wrigian*, to turn, go, move]; turned or twisted toward one side; askew; amiss; wrong. "Your crown's awry." (Shakespeare) |
| BAFFLEMENT | 3. | [LS. *bauchle*, also F., OF., Sp., It., H., etc., to scoff at, jeer]; state of being helplessly puzzled or thwarted; impediment or obstruction (of a solution); frustration. |
| BEATITUDE | 2. | [F. *béatitude*, L. *beatitudo, beatus*, happy]; consummate bliss; blessedness. "He was in a beatitude, his mouth unaware that it was smiling." (Bennett) |
| BENEVOLENT | 3. | [L. *benevolens*, wishing well]; disposed to do good; kindly; charitable. "My mother always employed benevolent actions while she uttered uncharitable words." (Wharton) |
| BIPED | 1. | [L. *bipes, bi*, two+*pes, pedis*, foot]; a two-footed animal, as man. |
| BLATANT | 4. | [coined by Spenser as an epithet of detraction]; offensively obtrusive; demanding attention by vulgar ostentation or conduct; noisy; clamorous. |
| BRONCHIAL | 4. | [G. *bronkhos*, windpipe]; of or pertaining to the windpipe and its branching tubes. |
| BUFFOON | 2. | [L. *buffare*, to play tricks, puff out the cheeks]; a clown; merry-andrew; hence, any absurd or clownish jester. |
| CACOPHONY | 3. | [G. *kakos*, bad+*phone*, sound]; harsh or jarring sound; dissonance; harsh or unharmonious use of language. |
| CADGE | 3. | [F. *cage*, wicker basket]; to get by begging. |
| CAJOLED | 1. | [F. *cajoler*, to chatter like a caged jay]; to wheedle; to coax. "He could neither be cajoled nor terrified from his avowal of the truth." (Trench) |
| CANDID | 2. | [L. *candidus*, white, glowing, pure, guileless]; without pretense or reserve; open; frank; without prejudice; fair. "Let us be candid and speak our mind." (Goldsmith) |
| CANDOR | 1. | [L. *candere*, to glow, be white]; frankness of expression; straightforwardness; freedom from prejudice. |
| CARDIACAL | 3. | [G. *kardia*, heart]; pertaining to the heart, or figuratively, love. Now archaic: *cardiac* is preferred. |
| CEREBRUM | 4. | [L. *cerebrum*, brain]; the large rounded structure of the brain occupying most of the cranial cavity. |
| CHARY | 2. | [AS. *cearig*, careful, *cearu*, care]; reserved in respect to feeling or conduct; shy; hesitant; shy (of). ". . . the *chariest* maid." (Shakespeare) |
| CHERUBIM | 4. | [Heb. *kerubh*, angel]; members of the second order of angels, ordinarily symbolizing divine wisdom. "I knew that they were the cherubims." (Ezek. 10:20) |
| CHLORINE | 4. | [G. *khloros*, greenish-yellow]; a highly irritating, greenish-yellow gaseous halogen, capable of combining with nearly all other elements and used widely to purify water, or as a disinfectant, or as a bleaching agent. |
| CIRCUMSPECT | 3. | [L. *circumspectus*, pp. of *circumspicere*, to look around, take heed]; heedful of circumstances or consequences; prudent. "The wild passes practical for the . . . circumspect mule." (Prescott) |

| | | |
|---|---|---|
| CLANDESTINE | 4. | [L. *clandestine,* F. *clam,* in secret, after L. *intestinus,* inward, intestine]; furtive; concealed, usually for some secret or illicit purpose. "I obtained access by clandestine means." (Collins) |
| COGNOSCENTI | 4. | [L. *cognoscere,* to get to know]; persons of superior knowledge or taste; connoisseurs. "A person of the most refined taste; an absolute cognoscenti." (Mason) |
| CONCESSION | 2. | [L. *concedere,* concede]; act of yielding, granting, or conceding. Also any thing or point so conceded. "But . . . I believe concessions to evil always do fail." (Bright) |
| CONCURRENCE | 4. | [L. *concurrere,* to run together]; agreement in opinion; co-operation. "Except there be a lucky concurrence of a postday with a holiday." (Johnson) |
| CONGENITAL | 1. | [L. *com,* together+*genitus,* born]; existing at birth but not hereditary; a congenital defect. Having a specified character as if by nature. |
| CONSUMMATE (adjective) | 3. | [L. *consummare,* to accomplish, sum up]; of the highest quality; complete. "Little dinners, consummate and select." (Beaconsfield) |
| CONSUMMATE (verb) | 4. | [L. *consummare,* to accomplish, sum up]; to bring to completion. "Lysander was eager to consummate his victory." (Thirlwall) |
| DALLIANCE | 2. | [ME. *dalien,* AS. *dweligean,* to err, be foolish]; amorous or wanton play; fondling; dawdling. "The Earl's courtship of Elizabeth was anything but a gentle dalliance." (Motley) |
| DANDER | 2. | [origin unknown]; anger, temper. "When my dander is up, it's the very thing to urge me on." (Thackeray) |
| DEBONAIR | 4. | [OF. *de bon aire,* L. *bonus,* good, of good disposition]; suave; urbane; nonchalant; affable; gracious; genial; carefree; jaunty. "So buxom, blithe, and debonair." (Milton) |
| DEBOUCH | 3. | [F. *déboucher,* from L. *bucca,* mouth, cheek]; to emerge into a more open place; to issue. "The travellers debouched on the open plain on Aldington Frith." (Barham) |
| DEFENESTRATE | 4. | [L. *de,* from+*fenestra,* window]; to throw a person or thing out of a window. |
| DEGENERATED | 4. | [L. *degenerare,* to fall from one's ancestral quality] deteriorated. |
| DEMISE | 2. | [F. *demettre,* to put away, dismiss]; death. "The unexpected demise of the crown changed the whole aspect of affairs." (Macaulay) |
| DIAPHANOUS | 4. | [G. *diaphainein,* to show or shine through]; having a texture so delicate as to be transparent; like gossamer in delicacy and fineness; translucent. |
| DILEMMA | 4. | [G. *di,* twice+*lēmma,* assumption]; a situation that requires one to choose between two equally balanced alternatives; a quandary. |
| DISDAINFUL | 4. | [L. *de,* from+*dignāre,* to scorn]; full of, or expressing, disdain; scornful; contemptuous; haughtily indifferent, indignant; angry; hostile. |
| DISHEVELED | 1. | [OF. *deschevelle,* pp. of *descheveler,* to disarrange the hair]; rumpled; hanging in loose disarray; unkempt, as hair; disarranged; untidy. "In vehement diction, but disheveled grammar." (from *The Saturday Review*) |

| | | |
|---|---|---|
| DISPARAGE | 3. | [L. *dis*, negative+*parage*, rank]; to dishonor by a comparison with what is inferior; to depreciate; undervalue. "Thou durst not thus disparage glorious arms." (Milton) |
| DOTARD | 4. | [ME. *doteu*, to dope]; one whose mind is impaired, esp. by the second childhood of age. |
| DROVES | 1. | [AS. *drīfan*, to drive]; a large mass of people moving or acting as a body. "Where droves, as at a city gate, may pass." (Dryden) |
| ECSTATIC | 4. | [OF. *extasie*, to put out of place, derange]; pertaining to, causing, or caused by, ecstasy; rapt; enraptured. "This ecstatic fit of love and jealousy." (Hammond) |
| EFFICACIOUS | 3. | [L. *efficere*, to effect]; capable of producing the desired result. "To provide efficacious securities against this evil." (Mill) |
| EGREGIOUS | 3. | [L. *egregius*, standing out from the herd]; outstandingly bad; blatant; outrageous. |
| ENERVATED | 3. | [L. *enervare*, to remove the sinews from]; deprived of strength; devitalized. "The enervated and sickly habits of the literary class." (Emerson) |
| EPITOME | 2. | [G. *epi*, upon+*temnein*, to cut, *epitemnein*, to cut short]; a summary of a book, article, or the like; an embodiment of an entire class or type. "The Church of St. Mark is an epitome of the changes of Venetian architecture from the tenth to the nineteenth century." (Ruskin) |
| ESCHEW | 4. | [OF. *eschiuver*, *eschiver*, to shun, avoid]; to abstain carefully from or shun; to keep clear of; avoid. "They must not eschew evil, but do good in the world." (Beveridge) |
| EUPHONIC | 3. | [G. *euphonos*, sweet-voiced]; agreeable to the ear. |
| EXPEDITE | 4. | [L. *expedire*, to free the feet, to extricate]; to accelerate the process or progress of; to facilitate; hasten; quicken. |
| FARRAGO | 2. | [L. *farrago*, mixed fodder for cattle, mash, medley]; a medley; a mixture; jumble. "A confounded farrago of doubts, fears, hopes." (Sheridan) |
| FEIGN | 4. | [L. *fingere*, to form, fashion, invent]; to represent by false appearance; to pretend; simulate; sham; dissemble. "She cannot feign; she scorns hypocrisy." (Brontë) |
| FERVID | 2. | [L. *fervere*, to glow, boil]; impassioned; zealous; intensely fervent; burning. Fervid loyalty. |
| FETTER | 3. | [G. *pede*, foot]; anything that confines or restrains; a restraint. "Passion's too fierce to be in *fetter*[s] bound." (Dryden) |
| FLAUNT | 2. | [Prob. Sca.; cf. Sw. *flanka*, to waver, Dan. *flink*, smart, brisk, *et al*.]; to show off; to exhibit ostentatiously; to be gaudily in evidence; to wave proudly. "The Miss Lambs might now be seen flaunt[ing] along the street in French bonnets." (Irving) |
| FLOUT | 3. | [Da. *fluiten*, OF. *flauter*, to play the flute, to jeer]; to show contempt for; scoff at; scorn. |
| FLUSTERED | 3. | [ME. *flastren*, akin to Ic. *flaustra*, to bristle]; fluster; to make nervous, to upset by confusing or befuddling. |
| FUNGIBLE | 4. | [L. *fungi*, to discharge]; interchangeable. "A certain number of persons do not regard books as fungible, but exercise a choice as to the books they read." (from *The Saturday Review*) |

| | |
|---|---|
| GAUDY | 3. [L. *gaudere,* to delight in]; characterized by tasteless show or showy colors; garish. |
| GLIBLY | 4. [MG. *glibberich,* slippery]; easily and fluently, esp. in speech or writing; superficially; insincerely. |
| GOURMAND | 2. [F. *gourmand,* glutton]; greedy or ravenous eater; glutton. ". . . that great gourmand, fat Apicius." (Jonson) |
| GOURMET | 4. [F. *gourmet,* epicure, winetaster]; a connoisseur in eating and drinking; an epicure. |
| GREGARIOUS | 4. [L. *gregarius,* belonging to a herd or flock]; seeking and enjoying the company of one's kind; sociable. |
| GUILE | 2. [MG. *guile, gile,* OF. *guile, guille,* AS. *wigle,* divination, sorcery]; crafty or deceitful cunning; duplicity; deceit; treachery. ". . . where guile and trickery and honorable ambition all struggled together." (Cather) |
| GUTTERSNIPE | 4. Slang; a person of the gutter, as a ragpicker or a street Arab. |
| HYPOCHONDRIAC | 2. [G. *hupokhondria,* pl. of *hupokhondrion,* belly, abdomen (formerly held to be the seat of melancholy]; a person neurotically convinced of illness. |
| ICONOCLAST | 3. [MG. *eikonoklastes,* image-breaker]; destroyer of sacred images; one who attacks and seeks to overthrow traditional or popular ideas or institutions. |
| IMMANENT | 2. [L. *im,* in+*manere,* to remain]; existing or remaining within; restricted entirely to the mind; subjective. |
| IMMINENT | 3. [L. *imminēre,* to project over or toward]; about to occur; impending. |
| IMPENDING | 2. [L. *impendere,* to weight out, pay]; to be about to happen; to be imminent. "Barbarism is ever impending over the civilized world." (J. H. Newman) |
| INCAPACITATE | 2. [F. *incapacité,* inability]; to deprive of natural power, capacity, or vigor; to disable. |
| INCREDIBLE | 2. [L. *incredibilis, in,* not+*credibilis,* credible]; unbelievable. |
| INDEFATIGABLE | 2. [L. *indefatigare, in,* not, *de,* from, *fatigare,* weary]; incapable of being fatigued or not yielding to fatigue. ". . . indefatigable champion." |
| INEDIBLE | 4. [L. *in,* not+*edere,* to eat]; not suitable for food, not edible. |
| INEXORABLE | 1. [L. *in,* not+*exorare,* to move]; not capable of being persuaded by entreaty; unyielding. "More fierce and more inexorable far/Than empty tigers or the roaring sea." (Shakespeare) |
| INEXPUNGEABLE | 3. [L. *in,* not+*expungere,* to mark for deletion]; not able to be blotted out or rubbed out; invincible. |
| INSINUATE | 2. [L. *in,* in+*sinus,* a bend, *insinuare,* to insinuate]; convey with oblique hints and allusions; hint covertly; suggest. Also introduce gradually and insidiously. |
| INTREPID | 3. [L. *in,* not+*trepidus,* fearful]; fearless; bold; brave; resolutely courageous. "Thinking is but the intrepid effort of the soul to keep the open independence of her sea." (Melville) |
| LACONIC | 1. [G. *Lakonikos,* of or resembling the Spartans (known for the brevity of their speech)]; terse; concise; succinct. "This cold, laconic note let down all Emma's hopes." (Hervey) |

| LATENT | 3. | [L. *latere*, to lie hidden or concealed]; not visible or apparent; dormant; hidden or concealed; present or existing but not exhibited or manifest. "The latent uncharitableness of men's minds." (Repplier) |
| LEERY | 3. | [AS. *hleor*, the cheek, the face, a look]; suspicious; distrustful; wary, knowing. "The old lady's a little leery of me, but I can win her all right." (Ade) |
| LENIENT | 2. | [L. *lenire*, to soothe]; merciful, restrained, or forgiving; gentle or understanding in disposition; not austere or strict; liberal; generous. "We have so much reason to be very lenient to each other." (Dickens) |
| LIVID | 4. | [L. *livere*, to be bluish]; having discolored skin, as from a bruise; of a leaden color, black and blue; extremely angry, furious. ". . . like the livid face of a drowned corpse at the bottom of a pool." (Conrad) |
| LOQUACIOUS | 4. | [L. *loqui*, to speak]; garrulous; talkative. |
| LUCID | 1. | [L. *lucere*, to shine]; clear; easily understood; sane. "The thought of Dante may be obscure, but the word is lucid or rather translucent." (Eliot) |
| LURID | 2. | [L. *luridus*, pallid, ghastly]; glowing or glaring through a haze; ghastly pale; causing shock or horror. "No lurid fire of hell or human passion illuminates their scenes." (Eliot) |
| MACHINATION | 4. | [L. *machinari*, to contrive, from *machina*, machine]; the act of plotting; a plot. "Ludlow escaped unhurt from the machination[s] of his enemies." (Macaulay) |
| MAGNANIMOUS | 3. | [L. *magnus*, great+*animus*, soul]; noble of mind and heart; generous in forgiving; above revenge or resentment; unselfish; gracious. |
| MALEVOLENT | 2. | [L. *male*, ill+*volens*, will, wish]; wishing evil or harm to others; malicious; having ill-will. |
| MALIGN | 3. | [L. *malignus*, evil-disposed]; evil in nature of intent; evil in influence; injurious; hateful. "Witchcraft may be by operation of malign spirits." (Bacon) |
| MANIACAL | 4. | [akin to G. *manesthai*, to rave]; affected with, or characterized by madness. |
| MEDIATOR | 3. | [L. *mediare*, to be in the middle]; a person or agent who serves as an intermediary in order to effect an agreement, settlement, compromise, or to reconcile differences between two or more conflicting parties. |
| MISANTHROPY | 4. | [G. *miso*, hate+*anthropos*, man]; hatred or dislike of mankind—not, as indicated in my verse, simply of men. |
| MISOGYNY | 4. | [G. *miso*, hate+*gyne*, women]; hatred of women. |
| MORBID | 4. | [L. *morbus*, disease]; susceptible to or preoccupied with gloomy or unwholesome matters; psychologically unhealthy. |
| MOTIVATION | 4. | [ME. *motif*, OF. *motif*, ML. *motivus*, moving]; inducement; incentive. |
| MYRIAD | 4. | [G. *myrios*, numberless]; countless; innumerable; multitudinous numbers. "Then came an old, dumb, myriad-wrinkled man." (Tennyson) |

| | | |
|---|---|---|
| NAÏVE | 2. | [L. *nasci*, to be born]; lacking worldliness and sophistication; artless; unaffected; simple and credulous as a child; ingenuous. "That naïve patriotism which leads every race to regard itself as evidently superior to every other." (Krutch) |
| NEFARIOUS | 3. | [L. *nefas*, crime, wrong]; wicked; evil; infamous. ". . . our politicians would not dare to sacrifice the life and happiness of innumerable children to their nefarious schemes." (Russell) |
| NEURALGIA | 2. | [G. *neuron*, nerve+*algia*, pain]; *Med.* an acute pain, constant or intermittent, radiating along the course of a nerve and its branches, also the morbid condition characterized by such pain. |
| NEUROSIS | 4. | [G. *neuron*, nerve+*osis*, process]; a functional nervous disorder without demonstrable physical lesion. |
| NOSTALGIA | 3. | [G. *nostos*, a return]; a longing for things, persons, or situations that are not present; homesickness. |
| OBSOLETE | 3. | [L. *obsolescere*, to fall into disuse]; disused as being antiquated. "A scientific textbook is obsolete in a decade or less." (Lowes) |
| OCULIST | 4. | [L. *oculus*, the eye]; a physician who treats diseases of the eye. |
| ODIUM | 4. | [L. *odi*, I hate]; 1. hatred, aversion; now, usually, state or fact of being hated. 2. the stigma attaching to what is hateful. "She threw the odium of the fact on me." (Dryden) |
| OMINOUS | 2. | [L. *ominosus*, from *omen*, sign, suffixed form of *o*, to announce, to hold as true]; of or pertaining to an omen; portentous; foreboding evil. "Ominous smiling silence." (Browning) |
| OPULENCE | 2. | [L. *opulentia*, from *opulentus*, rich]; wealth; riches, affluence, hence, plenty; amplitude. |
| OSCULATING | 2. | [L. *osculari*, to kiss]; kissing. |
| PALLID | 3. | [L. *pallere*, to be pale]; having an extremely pale or wan complexion; lacking intensity of color; dull; lifeless. "Consider . . . how pallid, and faint and dilute a thing, all the honors of this world." (Donne) |
| PANACEA | 2. | [G. *panakes*, all-healing]; a remedy for all diseases, evil, or difficulties; a cure-all. "Here was a panacea . . . for all human woes; here was the secret of happiness." (De Quincey) |
| PANOPLY | 2. | [G. *panoplia*, full suit of armor]; any bright or magnificent arrangement that forms a covering or protection; complete arms and armor of a warrior. |
| PARADOX | 2. | [G. *para*, beyond+*doxa*, opinion]; an assertion or sentiment seemingly opposed to common sense, yet perhaps true. "The old will perennially become new at the hand of genius. That is the paradox of art." (Lowes) |
| PATENT | 3. | [L. *patere*, to be open]; not hidden from eyes or mind; evident; obvious; manifest. "A patent fact, as certain as anything in mathematics." (Blackie) |
| PERSPICACITY | 4. | [L. *perspicere*, to see through]; acuteness of perception, dis- |

cernment, or understanding. "It was a marvelous effort of perspicacity to discover I did not love her." (E. Brontë)

PERVERSION 3. [L. *per vertere*, to turn through]; a turning from truth or right; deviance.

PHILANDER 3. [G. *philos*, love+*andros*, man]; to make love, esp. triflingly; to flirt. "I must disguise my sentiments, or I shall get none of the pretty fools to philander with." (Anon.)

PHILTRUM 3. [G. *philtron*, to love]; the vertical groove on the median line of the upper lip.

PHILEGMATIC 3. [G. *phlegmatikos*, having phlegm]; sluggish, not easily aroused or moved; apathetic; calm; composed. "His joy and his grief . . . were hidden by a phlegmatic serenity." (Macaulay)

PICAYUNISH 1. [F. *picaillon*, small copper coin]; of little value; petty; paltry; mean; as a picayunish business. Also narrow, as in outlook or policy.

PODIUM 3. [L. *podium*, an elevated platform, balcony]; a dais as for an orchestra conductor or speaker.

POSTHUMOUS 3. [L. *posthumus*, the last born]; following or occurring after death. "We should be contented with posthumous fame." (Southey)

PRESAGES 4. [L. *praesagire*, to perceive beforehand]; predicts; forecasts; augurs; gives an omen or warning. "The rising of the mercury presages, in general, fair weather." (Imison)

PREVALENT 2. [L. *praevalere*, to prevail]; widely or commonly occurring or existing; widespread; prevailing; generally accepted or practiced.

PROFANE 3. [L. *profanus*, outside the temple, hence secular]; unholy, showing contempt or irreverence toward God or sacred things; blasphemous; nonreligious in subject matter, form, or use; secular, vulgar; coarse. "I have observed that profane men living in ships, like the holy men gathered together in monasteries, develop traits of profound resemblance." (Conrad)

PROGENY 4. [L. *progignere*, to beget]; offspring; issue; specif. descendants, children collectively. "From this union sprang a vigorous progeny." (Hawthorne)

PROPAGATE 3. [L. *propagare*, to propagate plants by means of slips]; to cause animals or plants to multiply or breed; to breed offspring. Also to make known; publicize. "Motion propagated motion, and life threw off life." (De Quincey)

PROPHYLACTIC 3. [G. *prophulassein*, to stand on guard, take precautions against]; *Med.* device or measure that acts to defend against or prevent something, especially disease; a protective; in common usage a condom.

PRURIENCE 4. [L. *pruriens*, *prurire*, to itch]; lascivious desire or thought; lecherous imagination. ". . . the pruriency of curious ears." (Burke)

PUBESCENTS 3. [L. *pubescens*, to reach puberty]; young people at puberty; adolescents.

PUGNACITY 2. [L. *pugnare*, to fight]; eagerness or inclination to fight; combativeness; belligerency.

QUAY 2. [OF. *chai*, *cay*, Gaulish *caio*, rampart, retaining wall]; a wharf or reinforced bank where ships are loaded or unloaded.

QUIETUS    2.   [L. *quietus*, at rest, quiet]; that which silences claims; hence by extension, discharge from office, duty, or life; hence, death, also death blow. "When he himself might his quietus make with a bare bodkin." (Shakespeare)

RANDOM    3.   [OF. *randon*, violence, rapidity]; without definite aim or method, as haphazard.

REALISTIC    3.   [L. *res*, thing]; characterized by artistic or literary realism; representing things as they really are; concerned with a practical view of life.

REGENERATED    2.   [L. *regenerare*, to reproduce]; spiritually or morally revitalized; restored; refreshed; renewed.

REPULSIVE    4.   [L. *repellere*, to repel]; serving, or able, to repulse or repel; arousing aversion or disgust; offensive; repellent. "Balzac is often repulsive, and not infrequently dull." (Stephens)

RETROSPECT    4.   [L. *retrospicere*, to look back]; a reference to some precedent or past time; a view or survey of some past course of events, acts, esp. with reference to one's own life or experience.

RHADAMANTHINE    2.   Of or pertaining to, or characteristic of Rhadamanthus [judge of the underworld in Greek myth]; rigorously just. "Severe, rhadamanthine judges are not to be melted by such trumpery." (Thackeray)

RIBALD    2.   [OHG. *hriba*, prostitute]; blasphemous; obscene; coarsely offensive in language. "A ribald folk song about fleas in straw." (Lowes)

SACRILEGIOUS    4.   [L. *sacrilegus*, one who steals sacred things]; disrespectful or irreverent toward anything regarded as sacred; impious; profane.

SCRUPULOUSLY    2.   [L. *scrupulosis*, precise]; conscientiously, precisely, punctiliously. "An elderly woman, somewhat rough-looking but scrupulously clean." (C. Brontë)

SEDATELY    2.   [L. *sedare*, to settle, allay]; calm; quiet; composed; coolly, soberly, collectedly; undisturbed by passion or excitement. "John looked sedately and solemnly at his questioner." (Dickens)

SEMANTIC    4.   [G. *semantikos*, significant]; pertaining to meaning in language.

SIMULATE    4.   [L. *similis*, similar]; to assume the appearance, form, or sound of; imitate; to make a pretense of; feign. "He did not think it worth his while to simulate regret for his errors." (Macaulay)

SINEW    4.   [AS. *sinu*, tendon]; tendon. Also vigorous strength, muscular power. "Justice, which is the chief sinew of society." (Burnet)

SLANDER    2.   [L. *scandalum*, scandal]; in law, utterance of defamatory statements injurious to the reputation of a person. Also a malicious statement or report. "The envious reduces his rivals to despair by his unjust slanders of them." (Jowett)

SORDID    3.   [L. *sordere*, to be dirty]; dirty; foul; wretched; squalid; morally degraded; vile; extremely mercenary. "To scorn the sordid world." (Milton)

STATISTIC    2.   [NL. *statisticus*, of state affairs, from L. *status*, position, state]; a numerical datum.

| | | |
|---|---|---|
| SUCCINCT | 2. | [L. *succingere*, to gird below, tuck up, *sub*, below+*cingere*, to gird]; concise; terse; characterized by brevity and clarity in speech. "A strict and succinct style is that where you can take away nothing without loss, and that loss to be manifest." (Johnson) |
| SUPERSEDE | 3. | [L. *supersedere*, to sit above, desist from]; to take the place of; replace or succeed; to cause to be set aside or displaced. |
| SYCOPHANTIC | 2. | [G. *sukophantikos*, accuser, hence informer, flatterer]; like one who attempts to win favor or advancement by flattering persons of influence; with a servile manner. "A sycophant will everything admire;/Each verse, each sentence, sets his/soul on fire." (Dryden) |
| TACITURN | 4. | [L. *tacitus*, silent]; habitually untalkative; laconic; uncommunicative. |
| TANDEM | 3. | [L. *tandem*, at length (of time) used punningly]; one after another or behind another. |
| THEORETICAL | 2. | [G. *theoretikos*, able to perceive]; pertaining to or based on theory; lacking verification or practical application; speculative; unproved. |
| TINGLE-AIRY | 4. | A hand organ. |
| TYRO | 3. | [L. *tiro*, a newly levied soldier, a beginner]; a beginner in learning; a person imperfectly acquainted with a subject; a novice. "It will be advisable for a tyro in composition to look over what he has written." (Whately) |
| UXORIOUS | 4. | [L. *uxorious, unor*, wife]; excessively or irrationally fond of, or submissive to, a wife. "I am a little what vulgar folks call uxorious and am never truly eloquent upon any subject but my wife and children." (Wakefield) |
| VACILLATE | 4. | [L. *vacillare, vacillatum*]; to waver in mind, will, or feeling; to hesitate in choice of opinions; to fluctuate in one's emotions, judgments, etc. "He may pause, but he must not hesitate; and tremble, but he must not vacillate." (Ruskin) |
| VERBOSE | 3. | [L. *verbosus, verbum*, word]; using or containing more words than are necessary; hence tedious speech; prolix; wordy; as, a verbose speaker. |
| VIRAGO | 1. | [L. *virago*, from *vir*, man. Virago is applied now only to women; I think of no comparable word in English for a man.]; a termagant; a vixen; a scold. "The lust of power turned some of them into unsexed viragos, like Antony's Fulvia." (Buchan) |
| WANTON | 3. | [ME. *wantowen*, lacking discipline, lewd]; unchaste; immoral; lewd; maliciously cruel; freely extravagant. "The wanton troopers riding by/Have shot my Faun and it will die." (Marvel) |

A bustard whose diet was carrion, 133

A choir boy, when hymns became tedious, 145

A cub said, "My rump was just smackted, 170

A giraffe, thinking hay would be edible, 134

A lady with a laughing eye, 159

A maxim once true, 191

A mouse that hounds a cat about, 147

A Neolith of the name of Smith, 12

A Parrot (gaudy, debonair), 139

A passing lion reassured a bull, 135

A quay's pronounced like key; some day, 180

A sweet young thing's my true love, 70

A whore said, "I couldn't care less, 92

A wicked fellow lured a chit, 132

Abbreviations need a ma, 71

Aboard, Laertes, and my blessings carry, 84

Affluence and opulence, 130

Alike in sound are immanent, 132

Although, 183

Although informal speech is free, 155

An atheist at heaven's gate, 116

An ATHlete and an ATH-e-lete are in my class at school, 170

"Be MOD-ren," says she, 178

Be warned, when Bruin's lips retract, 4

Best plump for inconsistency, 157

Brothers twain combat each other, 191

By day and night, 187

"Can I become a man?" asks Little Bill, 195

Capable and able one may justly interchange, 189

Cries wife, "Go quick!" Cries wife, "Go slow," 197

Dangle, dangle, little stray, 191

Data are not singular, 191

Dear comrades, let us all together to the barman cry, 187

Dear wife, dear brother, sister, pal, 16

Dear youth: With gnarling fingers I indict, 80

Dog, go bite, 177

Don't disparage, 122

Don't eat like a pig!—you're, 174

Dribble a scribble a, 90

Dull was I—as apathetic, 136

E-PIT-o-mē is kind and fair, 173

Except (a verb that means "leave out"), 85

Fairy godma, make her kiss stick, 121

Fella in a hash house, musta been a waiter, 179

Folks who say "Jog-ger-fy," 175

For "height," you keep on saying "heighth," 101

For those who wish to dodge any, 124

Former, latter, are in sum, 192

Gen, when I'm in the dumps, 140

Get gets around. Get also gets the air, 58

Good pal, how glibly you proceed, 138

He said that he loved only me, 196

Hirohito's riding by, 54

How naïve, 134

I can prove by Holy Writ, 123

I didn't know quite what my
chum meant, 176
I do not know, or care, if you,
182
I don't think a porgy, 179
I feel for you when you
complain, 177
I have a little philtrum, 118
I have heard your friends
insinu-, 148
I have two little helpers whom I
love as kin and kith, 152
I hear that IM-po-tence is tough,
177
I know a fella, 183
I lack perspicacity, 138
I may do what you ban not,
195
I met a man, 100
I offered Emmy, 100
I once knew a gander, 127
I prayed, "One kiss, O fairest of
thy sex, 14
I preen myself on my
mustache, 153
I saw her through a magic prism,
182
I seldom rest beneath a bough,
98
I sorrow, as this bed we rest in,
172
I told a dragon, "You're
anachronistic, 141
I was casketed to bury, 174
I wish that my troubles were
fewer, 192
I wooed you in phrases laconic,
135
I'd say, in retrospect, you, 127
If comparatives you double, 158
If he says ellum, 173
If you and Oates, 195
If you hear a man who cries,
181
If you say awful, 188
Ike, asked why, 178
I'll bring you a bottle of prime
Beaujolais, 189
"I'm a poor blea—, 180
I'm an ancient one, 199

I'm chary of the look of you,
119
"I'm nauseous," to be precise,
84
In France, a fly s'appelle une
mouche, 118
In the beginning was the Word,
xvii
In this brief poem, there will be,
83
In words with double C's,
express, 169
"Increasingly more," 193
Iniquity . . . uniquity, 83
It is preferable to, 180
It's all to the good to be all ears,
58
It's safe to dis-re-gard the guy,
194
Jack says AV-vi-a-tor, 170
Jim asked her, "Do you love me
more, 193
Let me speak with candor, 144
Let prurience among pubescents,
126
Let us play at add-a-word, 115
Lie down once more where once
we kissed, 198
Love's my sickness; offer me a,
142
Lucky Si! his Siwash love, 42
Machine—ma-SHĒN. Yet
machination, 178
Malevolent, 146
Medora, the lioness down at the
zoo, 148
Michael's bicycle, 171
My idol!—your idle, 86
My lovin' sugar daddy, 181
My neighbor John, who cheats,
182
My pitcher and my picture I can
hardly tell apart, 86
My tongue can't handle "Amn't
I," 187
None recalls that I am there,
128
Of that iconoclast beware, 141
Once, astride a pony pie-bald,
181

One alternates at will (or shall,
200

One fury alone I have found
inexpungeable, 130

Pray take this apothegm along,
124

Reassure, 173

Said a gourmand to a gourmet,
120

Said a hooker who works out of
Niles, 91

Said Mary to Eddy, 187

Sir Galahad was strong as ten,
101

Slap like a midge a, 101

Slaughta, 179

Smardy, smardy, had a pardy,
100

Some IM-pi-ous old scoundrels
may, 177

Sorry—owing to, 175

"Status" doesn't rhyme with "pat
us"—, 182

Staying at the Claridge, 175

Such brooding beauty I discern,
136

SYL- is for Silly, 159

The boy who said
"ig-NOM-in-y," 176

The cat, who was flustered, 147

The chap who says CRON-ik-l,
172

The day the man who seeks to
justify, 190

The ə on his diurnəl rounds, 169

The English neigh, in voices gay,
196

The faults you complain of in
me, 92

The first part of April, it rained,
188

The heaving of her maiden
breast, 85

The laddies in droves upon
Betty call, 143

The man who speaks of
JEN-yoo-īne, 175

The owl that says "to-whit,
to-who," 194

The tears that fell at your

demise, 130

The television tube doth treat
us, 131

The verse you write, 156

The worker striking for a rise,
198

There's but one, 153

They laughed, back home, 179

They powwow still in the woods
of spruce, 41

This item mark—a recipe, 54

Though Cal's appetite is meager,
192

Though loan's a noun (the verb
is lend), 194

Though men breathe oxygen, it
all, 137

Though VER-sa-til as seasons,
176

To her cer-EB-rum Ann refers,
171

To say mis-CHĒV-i-ous, 178

Unique, you say, 189

Unless you weed the pathways
neural, 196

Until his second lager, he, 183

We test all rules (so goes the
wheeze), 199

We will not receive a minus, 174

What bafflement is mine and
yours, 139

What? Do you in a thumbnail
sketch? I may go, 117

What I imply, I hint. What you
infer, 152

When baby's going beddy-bye,
134

When Cottontail's heartsy went
stopsy, 171

When I am you, and you are I,
111

When I am drinking on the sly,
133

When I for overdue promotion
buck, 145

When I speak, do faces shine,
100

When I was asked to choose
between, 188

When I was boss, I canned a,
196

When Jack was twenty-one or
such, 149

When our desire is so in spate,
86

When stomping foe recumbent,
199

When the moon is thin and
pallid, 142

When the time arrives to
costume us, 128

When the whole blamed
caboodle has gone up the
spout, 59

When you're ill, 192

Where Sierras rise from mesas,
43

While still agile, I'll eschew, 125

With quizzic brow, or lashes
lowered, 6

You are just a gutter-snipe, Ed,
119

You are scarce turned twenty,
Algy—a, 123

You have toped too mush, in
faith, 173

You say KEW-pon, meaning
COOP-on, 172

You say 'leven for eleven, 173

Your charms, my dear, though
myriad, 129

Your eyes are different *than*
mine, 153

Your iguana, I can tell, 101

Your "width" sounds very much
like "with," 101

## FIRST LINES OF VERSES BY OTHER AUTHORS

All day she hurried to get
through, 31

A man sat on a rock and sought,
6

A muvver was barfin' 'er biby
one night, 23

A Russian sailed over the blue
Black Sea, 50

Ay ant lak pie-plant pie so wery
vell, 48

A young man called
Cholmondeley Colquhoun, 20

Blow, blow thou, 17

Der Spring is sprung, 32

Der vhas a leedle voman once,
46

'Er as was 'as gone from we, 26

Geeve a leesten mine cheeldren
you'll gonna hear, 51

Hans Breitmann give a barty, 45

Hermit hoar, in solemn cell, 1

If-itty-thesi-mow Jays, 53

I gotta love for Angela, 55

I laughingly replied, " 'Tis
tyrannical dealing," 18

I like to lie down in the sun, 25

Infinitesimal James, 53

In good King Charles's golden
days, 18

I rang the bell and I said to him,
53

I thought the winner had been
found, 32

Jejune, transpire, ilk, demean,
77

Joe Baratta's Giuseppina, 49

Last year my look-see plum-tlee,
53

Little Orphant Annie's come to
our house to stay, 34

Oh, I am a cook, and a captain
bold, 12

On yonder hill there stands a
coo, 26

Po' li'l fly, 37

Qvite horfen, fer a lark, coves
on a ship, 24

Remember when hippy meant
big in the hips, 76

Say there! P'r'aps, 35

Seen my lady home las' night,
37

Superintendent wuz Flannigan,
47

The pronunciation of Erse, 21
There was a young curate of
   Salisbury, 20
The verse you write, 156
Tomorrow I'll, 33
'Twas on a Monday morning, 25

We 'ad a little outing larst
   Sunday afternoon, 22
Within the bond of marriage, tell
   me, Brutus, 70
You can pass on de wor'
   w'erever you lak, 43

801